Gracias
Sr.

COMFORT WOMAN

COMFORT WOMAN

A Filipina's Story of Prostitution and Slavery under the Japanese Military

Second Edition

Maria Rosa Henson

ROWMAN & LITTLEFIELD
Lanham • Boulder • New York • London

Published by Rowman & Littlefield
A wholly owned subsidiary of
The Rowman & Littlefield Publishing Group, Inc.
4501 Forbes Boulevard, Suite 200, Lanham, Maryland 20706
www.rowman.com

Unit A, Whitacre Mews, 26-34 Stannary Street, London SE11 4AB,
United Kingdom

British Library Cataloguing in Publication Information Available

The first edition of this book was previously cataloged by the Library of
Congress as follows:
Henson, Maria Rosa, 1927–
Comfort woman: a Filipina's story of prostitution and slavery under the
    Japanese military / Maria Rosa Henson
p. cm.
1. Comfort woman—Philippines—History. 2. Prostitution—Philip-
    pines—History. 3. World War, 1939–1945—Women—Atrocities. 4.
    World War, 1939–1945—Asia—Atrocities. I. Title.
D810.C698H47 1999
940.53'081'09599 dc21
98—52031

ISBN 978-1-4422-7354-2 (cloth : alk. paper)
ISBN 978-1-4422-7355-9 (pbk. : alk. paper)
ISBN 978-1-4422-7356-6 (electronic)

∞ ™ The paper used in this publication meets the minimum require-
ments of American National Standard for Information Sciences Perma-
nence of Paper for Printed Library Materials, ANSI/NISO Z39.48-1992.

Printed in the United States of America

CONTENTS

FOREWORD

Cynthia Enloe

Decisions. There are always decisions. We sometimes don't bother to look for them. We often don't initially know where to look for them. Worse still, we lazily imagine that what has happened didn't even require decisions. It "just happened." Or the mere passage of time created it. Or it is the product of culture. Or of "circumstances."

These are dangerous assumptions. Each of them weakens our capacity for causal analysis. Together, they breed unaccountability. Impunity thrives on our lazy assumptions. Weak causal analysis, unaccountability, impunity—together, they make it all too likely that we will repeat the worst mistakes of recent history.

Feminist investigatory approaches have many advantages, one of the foremost being that they eschew laziness; they pursue not just impacts, but also causes. A feminist-informed perspective, such as that adopted here by historian Yuki Tanaka in his introduction to *Comfort Woman*, looks hard for decisions—and names the decision makers.

The more informed any investigation is by feminist curiosity, the less likely it is to nurture unaccountability and impunity.

Nowhere has a lazy inattention to decisions and decision makers, this lack of energetic curiosity, been more risky than in the interlinked politics of militarization, war waging, militarized prostitution, and militarized rape. "The oldest profession" is conventionally wielded, casually and arrogantly, to explain—to explain away—the existence of particular wartime systems of prostituting certain women in order to provide certain militarized men with commercialized sexual access to those women. "The oldest profession" makes a feminist-informed investigator's skin crawl. The implication is that any particular system of prostitution (peacetime or wartime) is merely part of an "age-old" human condition. It is thereby relegated to the timeless, to the unaccountable. "The oldest profession" is a phrase wielded with the intent of deadening curiosity and sustaining patriarchal impunity.

In this new edition of Maria Rosa Henson's powerful and courageous memoir, Yuki Tanaka brings the ongoing bitter battles over the comfort woman issue up to the present.

The book is being published at an historical moment when the gendered dynamics of militarism are particularly salient—not only in Japan, but also in South Korea, North Korea, Vietnam, the Philippines, the United States, and China. World War II history is not "back then." It is now, because understandings of what happened to whom by whom and why are shaping how we each make sense of the current resurgence of militarism in Asia.

Every revelation about, every interpretation of, every denial of the 1930s to mid-1940s militarized prostitution systems is fraught with meaning today. We had better understand it with evidence and with our eyes wide open. Especially as we are reminded of its deeply human, personal, and individual costs.

PREFACE

Sheila S. Coronel

ROSA HENSON wrote this biography by hand on sheets of lined paper for about a year. There were times, she said, when the memories were so fresh and so raw that she cried as she wrote. But she knew that she had to tell her story. It was Yuki Shiga-Fujime, a professor of contemporary history at Kyoto University, who first encouraged Lola Rosa to put her story in writing and patiently worked with her through the first drafts of this work.

Yuki translated the biography in Japanese and launched it in Japan in January 1996.

Lola Rosa showed us her manuscript in late 1995, and we knew immediately that it was an invaluable work. We helped her with some revisions, did some editing and divided the work into readable chapters. The structure and the language, however, are essentially Lola Rosa's. The illustrations are entirely hers as well. The subtitle of the Japanese edition, "Slave of Destiny," was also her idea.

Comfort Woman is a story of Rosa Henson's courage and determination to survive. It is a story that has moved us deeply. This woman has true grit, and her strength inspires us all.

INTRODUCTION

Yuki Tanaka

Exactly when the Japanese Imperial Forces first set up *ianjo* ("comfort stations," or military brothels) for the exclusive use of their soldiers and officers is unknown, because a vast number of relevant official records were destroyed immediately after Japan announced its surrender in August 1945. However, a number of official Japanese government and military documents related to this issue were unearthed in the late 1980s and early 1990s.[1] Information available in these newly discovered documents strongly suggests that the first Japanese military-run brothels were those set up for the Japanese navy in Shanghai during the Shanghai Incident in early 1932.[2]

The Japanese army followed the navy's precedent, setting up its own brothels in Shanghai in March 1932. These were initiated by General Okamura Yasuji, the deputy chief of staff of the Shanghai Expeditionary Army. According to his memoirs, the general decided to set up facilities similar to those recently established by the navy in order to prevent the further rape of Chinese civilians by Japanese soldiers, a serious problem during the Shanghai Incident. General Okamura asked the governor of Nagasaki Prefecture in Kyushu to send a group of "comfort women" to Shanghai.[3] His choice of Nagasaki as a recruiting center for these women was probably historically based.

Many so-called *karayuki-san* (women travelers) of poor family background had previously been sent from Nagasaki to various places throughout the Asia-Pacific region where Japanese expatriates resided. It is clear from Okamura's private records that, at this stage, the army intended to use professional Japanese prostitutes.

Although the Japanese set up a number of comfort stations in Shanghai and in northeast China in the early 1930s, it was not until 1937, shortly after Japan embarked on full-scale war with China, that the Japanese Imperial Forces adopted the military brothel system as a general policy. The sudden increase in the number of Japanese military brothels in China was closely related to atrocities that Japanese soldiers committed during the Nanjing Massacre. In 1937, Japanese troops fought a fierce battle in Shanghai (the Second Shanghai Incident), which lasted three months. Following that battle, Japan's Central China Area Army, led by General Matsui Iwane, advanced in early November 1937 toward Nanjing. Members of this army committed crimes such as looting, killing, arson, and rape at various places along the Yangtze River on their way to Nanjing.

They continued on their spree after entering the city, an incident that has become known as the Nanjing Massacre. The leaders of the Central China Area Army quickly recognized the seriousness of the problem of mass rape committed by their soldiers. Thus, on December 11 they instructed the commanders of each military contingent to set up military brothels in order to prevent further rapes.[4] As a result, from early 1938, comfort stations were set up at almost all places where Japanese troops were stationed outside the home islands. A large number of Korean and Chinese women were mobilized as comfort women.

After the outbreak of the Pacific War in December 1941, the comfort woman system was expanded to other war zones and to occupied territories in the vast Asia-Pacific region. According to one document prepared by the Ministry of War in September 1942, 400 comfort stations were operating at the time—100 in north China, 140 in central China, 40 in south China, 100 in

Southeast Asia, 10 in the southwest Pacific, and 10 in
Sakhalin.[5]

There were four major reasons why Japanese military ...
created the comfort woman system. First, it was a means to reduce
the rape of civilians by members of the Japanese armed forces at
war in China. The Nanjing Massacre revealed the seriousness of
the problem of the rape of Chinese women by Japanese forces.
Military leaders were deeply concerned that such serious crimes
by Japanese armed forces would arouse the antagonism of civilians
toward their conquerors in the occupied territories and believed
that a ready supply of women for the troops would reduce the
incidence of rape. In other words, the system was introduced for
strategic reasons, not out of concern for civilians.

Second, military leaders believed that it was important to grat-
ify their men's carnal desires. Unlike U.S. and other Allied soldiers, the rank and file of the Japanese Imperial Forces had no
designated leave periods or limits on tours of duty. Military leaders had been advised by senior medical staff to provide more
wholesome amenities for the health and well-being of their men.
Most of the suggested measures were never adopted, with the
notable exception of the provision of comfort women.

Third, military-controlled prostitution was regarded as an effective preventive measure against venereal disease. High VD
rates among military troops were a common problem not only for
the Japanese Imperial Forces but also for the Allied forces
throughout the war and in the immediate postwar period. Military
leaders of both sides were concerned that VD threatened to
undermine the strength and morale, and hence the fighting abil-
ity, of their men. Japanese leaders also feared that the spread of
disease might create massive public health problems back in Japan
after the war. A regulated system such as comfort stations would
bring VD under control.

Finally, the tight control of brothels by the military authorities
was believed to be necessary for security reasons. It was feared
that private brothels frequented by military troops might easily be
infiltrated by spies. It was thought that prostitutes working in

.hem could also be recruited as spies by enemy forces. Members of the *kempeitai*—the Japanese military police—frequently visited comfort stations and kept close tabs on the women to ensure that there were no spies among them. For this purpose, the physical freedom of the comfort women was severely restricted.

To operate the brothels, large numbers of women were mobilized and exploited by the Japanese during the Asia-Pacific War. It is impossible to know exactly how many women were involved. However, it is estimated to be about a hundred thousand, 80 percent of whom are believed to have been Koreans. Many women from Taiwan, China, the Philippines, Indonesia, and Malaya were also pressed into sexual slavery. Women from Korea and Taiwan were particularly targeted; since these countries were Japanese colonies, the political and economic environment made it easier for the authorities to recruit. Many Japanese and Korean labor brokers, with support from the *kempeitai* and the civil police force in those countries, sought out suitable women. From various testimonies, including those of former Korean comfort women, there is no doubt that many of these labor brokers used dubious methods, such as deception, intimidation, violence, and even kidnapping.

In this way, the Japanese Imperial Forces exploited large numbers of Asian women under the pretext of preventing rape and VD. It must be noted, however, that the provision of comfort women was not an effective measure for resolving either problem. This is particularly so in the case of random sexual violence against civilians in occupied territories. Moreover, it should not be forgotten that despite official justifications for the program, the estimated hundred thousand women involved in the comfort women system were themselves victims of sexual violence and sexual slavery.[6]

FILIPINA VICTIMS OF THE COMFORT WOMEN SYSTEM

Several official documents that refer to comfort stations in the Philippines have been found in archives in Japan and the United States. According to one of these documents, in Manila alone, in early 1943, there were seventeen comfort stations for rank-and-file soldiers, "staffed" by 1,064 comfort women. In addition, there were four officers' clubs served by more than 120 women. No information is available as to the nationality of these women. Other documents reveal that comfort stations were also located at Iloilo on Panay Island, Butsuan and Cagayan de Oro on Mindanao Island, Masbate on Masbate Island, and Ormoc and Tacloban on Leyte Island. It is almost certain that there were comfort stations at many other places in the Philippines. These documents reveal little information about the women, but a few, such as those referring to comfort stations in Iloilo, mention a number of Filipina comfort women, including several girls between sixteen and twenty years old.[7] It is almost impossible to know from the archival documents how these women were "recruited" and under what conditions they were forced to serve the Japanese troops.

Some evidence and testimony presented at the International Military Tribunal for the Far East, which was conducted in Tokyo between May 1946 and November 1948, reveal that various atrocities, including many incidents of rape, were committed by Japanese troops against civilians in the Philippines. The proceedings of the War Crimes Tribunals, conducted by the American military forces in Manila shortly after the war—such as the trial of General Yamashita Tomoyuki, the last commander of Japanese forces in the Philippines—also contain detailed reports on numerous cases of similar crimes committed by Japanese men. The evidence presented at these war-crimes trials was mainly related to cases that occurred either during the invasion of the Japanese forces into the Philippines, between late 1941 and early 1942, or toward the end of the Japanese occupation, in particular after October 1944, when U.S. forces landed on Leyte. Japanese brutality during the fierce battle in Manila in February 1945 is particularly well recorded. Yet little is known about the extent of sexual violence committed by the Japanese against civilians during the rest of the occupation period.

It was in 1992, more than a half century after the end of the war, that the truly horrific picture of this widespread sexual violence against Filipinas during the occupation first emerged. This was made possible when Maria Rosa Henson, the author of this autobiography, courageously came forward and revealed her painful past as a comfort woman. Encouraged by her action, many other women spoke out, one after another, and gave detailed testimonies about their wartime ordeals. Eventually, the testimonies of fifty-one women were collected by a local nongovernmental organization, called the Task Force on Filipino Comfort Women, together with a group of Japanese lawyers.[8]

The testimony of these Filipina victims makes clear that the "recruiting" methods that the Japanese troops employed in the Philippines were somewhat different from those used in other regions in the Asia-Pacific occupied by the Japanese Imperial Forces during the war, in particular Korea and Taiwan. The most common expedient used in Korea and Taiwan was deceit—false promises of employment in Japan or other Japanese-occupied territories. Typically, a daughter of a poor peasant family was approached by a labor broker and promised that she would be employed as an assistant nurse, kitchen helper, laundry worker, or something similar. She would not find out the real nature of the work until she was taken into a comfort station and raped by members of the Japanese armed forces.

Some women were sold to labor brokers by their parents (due to their desperate financial straits), eventually ending up at comfort stations somewhere in Southeast Asia or China. Some women testified that they were kidnapped by unknown civilians or arrested by police for no crime and then sent off to comfort stations overseas. In any case, in Korea and Taiwan, it was rare that military personnel were directly involved in recruiting women, which was usually carried out by Japanese or local labor brokers. In the

Dutch East Indies (now Indonesia), where the local population generally welcomed the entrance of the Japanese Imperial Forces into the territories as "liberators" from Dutch colonialism, it seems that deceit was also a common tactic employed by the Japanese to "recruit" local women. Forcible recruitment by intimidation or violence, such as the case of Dutch women and girls who were forcibly taken out of the detention camps in Java and pressed into service in comfort stations, was not a common method in this region.[9]

In contrast to the military authorities' behind-the-scenes approach in these regions, testimonies, including that of Maria Rosa Henson, indicate that in the Philippines the Japanese troops directly secured comfort women. Furthermore, their methods were wanton: abduction, rape, and continuous confinement for the purposes of sexual exploitation. It seems that the Japanese did not even try to conceal what they were doing to the civilians.

The main reason for such direct action by the Japanese troops in the Philippines may lie in the fact that the anti-Japanese guerrilla movement was strong and widespread throughout the occupation period. It is said that, at their peak, there were more than one hundred guerrilla organizations, involving about 270,000 activists and associates. Hukbalahap, which Maria Rosa Henson joined, was one of the largest of the guerrilla organizations. It was composed predominantly of peasants and workers under the influence of the Communist Party. As a result of this strong anti-Japanese movement, the Japanese were able to control only 30 percent of the Philippines. Guerrilla activities were particularly strong on Luzon and Panay.

The fact that the majority of the women who have so far been identified as former comfort women were residents of these two islands also indicates the close link between Japanese sexual violence against civilians and popular guerrilla activities. It is widely believed that in the Philippines the Japanese troops tended to regard any civilian as a possible guerrilla collaborator, and therefore they felt justified in doing anything to women "belonging to the enemy." Indeed, seven of the above-mentioned fifty-one victims testified that they were abducted by the Japanese during their guerrilla mopping-up operations. Similarly cruel treatment of local women by the Japanese can also be found near the front lines of the battle zones in China during the Asia-Pacific War.

In almost all of the fifty-one testimonies that have been collected, the victims were abducted by Japanese soldiers from home, work, or while walking in the street. In some cases, abductions were planned, but in many cases the women were simply picked up on the road by a small group of Japanese soldiers—as in the case of Maria Rosa Henson—and taken to a Japanese garrison nearby, where they were raped day after day. The duration of captivity was usually between one and several months. In a few cases, victims were confined for up to two years. In most cases, the premises where they were confined were part of the garrison compound or right next to it. They were guarded by Japanese soldiers twenty-four hours a day, which provided very little chance of escape. This was quite different from the typical comfort station in other parts of Asia, which in most cases was a facility completely separate from the barracks and managed by a Japanese or Korean civilian proprietor under the supervision of the military authorities.

In the Philippines, it seems that the usual practice was that about ten young women or girls were held by each small company-sized army unit for the exclusive exploitation of that unit. Most commonly, a victim was raped by five to ten soldiers every day. None of the victims was ever paid; some were forced to cook and wash for the Japanese soldiers during the day, then provide sexual services at night.

Another distinctive feature of comfort women in the Philippines is that they became victims of military sexual violence at very young ages. The average age in the comfort stations for which we have information is 17.6 years. Many were younger than fifteen years, and one was as young as ten years. Naturally, the younger girls had not yet begun to menstruate. An explanation for why the Japanese victimized such young girls will require further investigation.

Continuous rape in captivity was undoubtedly a tormenting experience for these women, but tragically some of these girls had had to endure the additional horror of witnessing the murder of their own parents and siblings by the Japanese at the time of their abduction. For example, one night in 1942, two Japanese soldiers invaded the home of thirteen-year-old Tomasa Salinog and her father in Antique on Panay Island. As two soldiers intruded, another two stayed outside on watch. Tomasa's father resisted the soldiers as they tried to take the child away. One of the Japanese, Captain Hirooka, suddenly drew his sword and severed the father's head. The Japanese soldiers dragged Tomasa out of the house, as she screamed at the sight of her father's head lying in the corner of the room.[10]

In another case, Rufina Fernandez, a seventeen-year-old Manila girl, witnessed the murder of both her parents and one of her sisters when Japanese soldiers broke into their home one night in 1944. The Japanese tried to take her and her father away with them. When he resisted, he was beheaded. When her mother tried to do the same, she was killed. Rufina's youngest sister was also killed. As Rufina was taken from the house, two other younger sisters were crying. Their crying suddenly stopped, and she presumed that they, too, had been killed.[11]

The overall picture that can be drawn from these testimonies is strikingly similar to the situation experienced by many women in Bosnia-Herzegovina during the Bosnian War of the early 1990s. The only notable difference is that the Japanese had no intention of deliberately making the girls pregnant as one method of "ethnic cleansing." The terms "comfort women" and "comfort station" are of course nothing but official euphemisms; readers of this autobiography will quickly discover the brutal reality of "comforting" Japanese soldiers. As with the Bosnian case, "rape camps" is probably a more appropriate term for the conditions of sexual enslavement into which many Filipinas and women from other regions in the Asia-Pacific were pressed.

FILIPINA CONTRIBUTIONS TO THE MOVEMENT AGAINST MILITARY VIOLENCE

In December 1991, a Manila-based nongovernmental organization, the Asian Women Human Rights Council (AWHRC), held a conference in Seoul on the issue of trafficking in Asian women. At this conference, some Korean participants raised the issue of comfort women. Prominent Filipina feminist activists such as Indai Sajor (coordinator of AWHRC) and Nelia Sancho heard for the first time about comfort women.

In March 1992, these women set up an organization called the Task Force on Filipino Comfort Women (TFFCW). It was a fact-finding group made up initially of seven women's organizations, including BAYAN-Women's Desk, Batis Centre for Women, National Council of Churches in the Philippines Women's Desk, and Women's Legal Bureau. Shortly afterward, the number of member organizations increased to fifteen, and the task force started searching for former comfort women. It was Maria Rosa Henson who first responded, in September 1992, when the TFFCW made a radio announcement asking former comfort women to come forward. One after another, women followed Maria's lead. Eventually, 169 women were identified as former comfort women.

Several Japanese lawyers, including Takagi Kenichi, Hayashi Yoko, and Yokota Yuichi, visited the Philippines to interview many of the women and record their testimonies. These lawyers were also working for former Korean comfort women who had sued the Japanese government for compensation. In April 1993 eighteen of these Filipina victims filed a lawsuit against the Japanese government at the Tokyo District Court, demanding an indemnity of twenty million yen per person from the Japanese state. Eventually, the number of plaintiffs increased to forty-six.

One of the legal bases of the claim is that Japan violated the Hague Convention of 1907, whose regulations protect civilians in occupied territories. The Japanese government had ratified the convention in 1912 and was thus bound by it when the Japanese Imperial Forces began attacks in the Philippines in late 1941.

Article 46 of the convention stipulates "respect for the reputation and rights of a family" and "of an individual life." This regulation clearly prohibits the violation of the basic rights of an individual as well as of his or her body. Furthermore, in most societies, sexual violence against a woman constitutes a serious violation of family honor and reputation. Rape and sexual abuse of women are thus a clear breach of Article 46 of the Hague Convention.

Another legal base is that the conduct of the Japanese troops in the Philippines clearly constituted "crimes against humanity," a notion officially defined and adopted in Article 6 of the International Military Tribunal Charter, which was established immediately after World War II. Since then, the concept of crimes against humanity has been repeatedly used in international law, such as the Convention on Genocide of 1948. Rape and other types of sexual violence are regarded as serious crimes against humanity by specialists on international law.

At a court hearing in Tokyo, only three of the forty-six plaintiffs were permitted to testify. Before the verdict was finally delivered—on October 9, 1998—four of the women had died. One of them was the author of this autobiography, Maria Rosa Henson. She passed away on August 18, 1997.

The Tokyo District Court dismissed the claims against the Japanese government filed by the Filipina victims. In summary, Judge Ichikawa Yoriaki's ruling was that the Hague Convention does not recognize the rights of individual victims to claim compensation against the state to which the occupying army belongs and that the notion of crimes against humanity is not an established part of the international customary law. However, Article 3 of the Hague Convention clearly states that "a belligerent party which violates the provisions of the said regulations shall, if the case demands, be liable to pay compensation. It shall be responsible for all acts committed by persons forming part of its armed forces."

As to the notion of crimes against humanity, it must be said that Judge Ichikawa is totally out of touch with current international trends. As Indai Sajor correctly pointed out in the statement she made shortly after the verdict was delivered, Ichikawa's judgment "has miserably fallen out of step with the worldwide effort by women and men to prosecute crimes in war and armed conflict situations, to the extent of working for the establishment of the International Criminal Court, which perceives gender-based prosecution during armed conflict situations as crimes against humanity and of which Japan is a signatory." After first being proposed in 1948, the establishment of an International Criminal Court was agreed to in July 1998 by 120 nations, including Japan. Since 1991 there have been a total of ten lawsuits against the Japanese government fielded by former comfort women—four Chinese (twenty-four plaintiffs), three Koreans (thirteen plaintiffs), one Taiwanese (nine plaintiffs), one Dutch (one plaintiff), and one Philippine (forty-six plaintiffs). Yet, all the cases were dismissed by the Japanese courts, either because of state exemption from responsibility to individuals or the relinquishment of a claim resulting from bilateral agreement between Japan and another foreign nation.

CONTEMPORARY REACTIONS OF THE JAPANESE GOVERNMENT AND NATIONALISTS

In order to allay worldwide criticism, in particular by Koreans, on August 4, 1993, the chief cabinet secretary of the Japanese government, Kono Yohei, issued a statement subsequently known as the Kono Statement, whereby the government officially admitted for the first time that the Japanese Imperial Forces were responsible for setting up the so-called comfort women system, i.e., a military sex-slave system, during the Asia-Pacific War. It reads in part:

> The Japanese military was, directly or indirectly, involved in the establishment and management of the comfort stations and the transfer of comfort women. The recruitment of the comfort women was conducted mainly by private recruiters who acted in response to the request of the military. The Government study has revealed that in many cases they were recruited

against their own will, through coaxing, coercion, etc., and that, at times, administrative/military personnel directly took part in the recruitments. They lived in misery at comfort stations under a coercive atmosphere.

Undeniably, this was an act, with the involvement of the military authorities of the day, that severely injured the honor and dignity of many women. The Government of Japan would like to take this opportunity once again to extend its sincere apologies and remorse to all those, irrespective of place of origin, who suffered immeasurable pain and incurable physical and psychological wounds as comfort women. [12]

The statement concluded by saying, "We hereby reiterate our firm determination never to repeat the same mistake by forever engraving such issues in our memories *through the study and teaching of history*"[13] (emphasis added). In accordance with this commitment, the Japanese government encouraged school textbook publishing houses to include references to the comfort women issue. As a result, from 1997 onward, all editions published by Japan's seven school-textbook publishing houses included references to the comfort women issue as well as other issues related to Japan's war responsibility in junior high school textbooks on Japanese history. Yet, the Japanese government did not and has still not admitted its *legal responsibility* for the surviving former sex slaves of the Japanese Imperial Forces. It is the government's consistent stance that all war compensation matters have been resolved with the 1965 Agreement between Japan and Korea Concerning the Settlement of Problems in Regard to Property and Claims and Economic Cooperation.

As a goodwill gesture, in July 1995, the Japanese government set up the Asian Women's Fund for the purpose of raising money from the private sector to be used for compensating former comfort women. This scheme clearly failed, as most of the victims refused to accept such "compensation" without Japan's official apology. Japan also rejected the 1995 Coomaraswamy Report, which recommended to the UN Commission on Human Rights that the Japanese government properly acknowledge its responsibility for the plight of the former comfort women. In August 1998, the McDugal Report to the same UN commission also urged Japan to correct its policy by officially compensating the victims. Yet, the Japanese government continues to turn a deaf ear to world opinion.

After 1996, certain nationalist politicians, academics, journalists, and right-wing political groups began a fierce campaign against these textbook reforms, claiming that the comfort women system was not a sex-slave system but a legitimate prostitution business arrangement. They strongly demanded that references to the comfort women issue be withdrawn from school textbooks. At the same time they also claimed that Japanese war atrocities such as the Nanjing Massacre were a Chinese fabrication and that the Japanese never committed such war crimes.[14] In June 1996, some hardliners from the LDP (Liberal Democratic Party) formed an organization called the Association of Parliamentarians for a Bright Japan. Abe Shinzo, the current prime minister, who had been elected as a member of the Lower House in the Diet (Japanese National Parliament) for the first time three years before, became the deputy secretary of this organization. In February 1997, this group was reorganized under the name of the Association of Young Parliamentarians for Japan's Future and Historical Education with an increased number of members. Again Abe became the secretary of this new organization. Together with Nakagawa Shoichi, the president of this association, Abe initiated a campaign within the Diet condemning Japanese education as "heavily biased."[15]

In an effort to counteract this misogynistic and nationalistic political campaign, an organization called Violence Against Women in War–Network Japan (hereafter VAWW–Net Japan) collaborated with other women's organizations throughout Asia to hold the Women's International War Crimes Tribunal on Japan's Military Sexual Slavery in Tokyo for five days in December 2000. About four hundred people from various parts of the world, including sixty-four former comfort women from eight different nations, participated in this people's tribunal, and every day more than a thousand people attended the trial. At this citizens' tribunal, many relevant official documents produced by the Japanese Imperial Forces as well as by the United States and other Allied military forces during and immediately after the war were presented as evidence for the crimes that the Japanese committed against numerous women. This documentary evidence was substantiated by the testimonies of a number of former comfort women and several former Japanese soldiers. As a result, Emperor Hirohito, General Tojo Hideki, and seven other Japanese top military leaders were indicted, and all were found guilty. The final judgment was issued in The Hague in December 2001. Yet, again, Abe, together with Nakagawa, exerted political pressure to sabotage the TV report on this tribunal produced by NHK (Japanese Broadcasting Corporation). As a result, the actual report broadcast was substantially diluted.

Due to continuous political pressure on textbook publishing houses by Abe, his nationalistic colleagues and politicians, as well as bureaucrats in the Ministry of Education, the number of history texts referring to the comfort women issue rapidly decreased within a few years. By 2006, no junior high school textbooks in Japan referred to the comfort women issue. All the publishers had bowed to implicit pressure of these conservative and nationalistic groups, choosing to eliminate the issue of comfort women in their textbooks.[16]

For many years Abe and his colleagues have been closely collaborating with nationalistic scholars such as Fujioka Nobukatsu, former professor of education at Tokyo University, one of the leading members of the group calling itself the Association for a Liberal View of History. On January 30, 1997, Fujioka and other members of this group formed another organization called the Association for Producing New Textbooks (*Atarashii Kyokasho o Tsukuru Kai*, hereafter APNT). In April 2004, APNT successfully submitted its own version of textbooks for Japanese history and social studies to the Ministry of Education for approval. Needless to say, these textbooks make no reference to any war crimes committed by the Japanese Imperial Forces throughout the Asia-Pacific. Instead, they justify Japan's military conduct and emphasize the superiority of the Japanese nation and culture. The APNT's textbooks were initially published by Fuyō Publishing House, a subsidiary of Fuji-Sankei Corporation, Japan's most conservative and nationalistic media (newspaper and TV) company, and are now published by two different right-wing publishing houses. The APNT has been gradually increasing the number of schools that adopt its textbooks. [17]

On September 26, 2006, Abe was elected as prime minister of Japan. On October 5 he stated in a Diet committee that there was no evidence to prove that comfort women were forcibly taken into comfort stations, so the issue must not be taught in junior high schools. Abe used the expression "coercion in the narrow sense" to indicate "abduction" or "kidnapping." By defining "coercion" simply as "abduction" and "kidnapping," he dismissed the fact that many women were deceived and conned into becoming sex slaves or sold to comfort stations because of poverty. [18] He ignored the role of the military in transporting women and girls, and organizing, controlling, and monitoring comfort stations throughout the Asia-Pacific. He also ignored cases such as that of Jan Ruff-O'Herne and other Dutch women who were forcibly taken from internment camps and put into comfort stations, a fact verified at the Dutch military war-crimes tribunal in 1948. Furthermore, his definition entirely dismisses many cases of such Chinese and Filipina victims as Maria Rosa Henson, the author of this autobiography, who were literally abducted and sexually enslaved by Japanese soldiers. It seems obvious that Abe adopted the concept of "coercion in the narrow sense" from the members of the group of nationalistic scholars such as Fujioka Nobukatsu, as well as from their distorted interpretation of the Tokyo War Crimes Tribunal.

In January 2007, Mike Honda, a member of the U.S. House of Representatives, proposed a resolution requesting that Japan "formally acknowledge, apologize, and accept historical responsibility in a clear and unequivocal manner for its Imperial Armed Forces' coercion of young women into sexual slavery, known to the world as comfort women, during its colonial and wartime occupation of Asia and the Pacific Islands from the 1930s through the duration of World War II."[19]

Concern for Honda's resolution proposal, as well as the anticipated reaction to it in the United States during his planned official visit there ten days later, undoubtedly led Abe to state on March 16, 2007, that he would respect the Kono Statement. He added, however, that it was confirmed at a cabinet meeting that there was no evidence in the documents found by the Japanese government to prove that women were forcibly taken away by Japanese military forces or police.

On March 24, 2007, the *Washington Post* sharply criticized Abe's attitude toward the comfort women issue as "double talk." It read in part, "What's odd and offensive is . . . to roll back Japan's acceptance of responsibility for the abduction, rape and sexual enslavement of tens of thousands of women during World War II. Responding to a pending resolution in the U.S. Congress calling for an official apology, Mr. Abe has twice this month issued statements claiming there is no documentation proving that the Japanese military participated in abducting the women. . . . He should straightforwardly accept responsibility for Japan's own crimes and apologize to the victims he has slandered."[20] The *New York Times* and many other newspapers in Korea, China, Taiwan, and the Philippines ran similar articles criticizing Abe's duplicity.

On March 27, 2007, Abe met U.S. president George W. Bush at Camp David. At the press conference after this meeting, Abe said, "Well, in my meeting with the congressional representatives yesterday, I explained my thoughts, and that is I do have deep-felt sympathy that many people had to serve as comfort women, were placed in extreme hardships, and had to suffer that sacrifice; and that I, as Prime Minister of Japan, expressed my apologies, and also expressed my apologies for the fact that they were placed in that sort of circumstance. The 20th century was a century when human rights were violated in many parts of the world. So we have to make the 21st century a century, a wonderful century in which no human rights are violated. And I, myself, and Japan wish to make significant contributions to that end. And so I explained these thoughts to the President." Bush replied to this by saying, "The comfort women issue is a regrettable chapter in the history of the world, and I accept the Prime Minister's apology. I thought it was very, I thought his statements, Kono's statement, as well as statements here in the United States were very straightforward and from his heart. And I'm looking forward to working with this man to lead our nations forward. And that's what we spent time discussing today. We had a personal visit on the issue. He gave his, he told me what was on his heart about the issue, and I appreciated his candor. And our jobs are to, obviously, learn lessons from the past. All of us need to learn lessons from the past and lead our nations forward. That's what the Prime Minister is doing in a very capable way."[21] It is extraordinary that Japan's prime minister, who had for years worked to suppress the issue of comfort women and deny Japanese government and military responsibility for the system, expressed apologies on the comfort women issue in the United States, and that the U.S. president accepted his apology while both completely ignored the actual victims of the Japanese military sex enslavement.

Abe has never expressed his apologies directly to any former comfort women since this meeting with Bush at Camp David in March 2007. When the House of Representatives passed Honda's resolution on July 30, 2007,[22] Abe simply said "it was disappointing."

Although initially Abe was prime minister for less than a year when he resigned on August 27, 2007, he returned to power on December 26, 2012. Since then, he has continued to deny the historical facts of the sexual enslavement of numerous women by the Japanese Imperial forces during the Asia-Pacific War.

One such political maneuver was "the review of the Kono Statement." The Abe cabinet suddenly made an announcement in February 2014 that it would review the Kono Statement by examining testimonies given by former Korean comfort women, which were used in the drafting of the Kono Statement issued in August 1993. At the same time, however, in an attempt to avoid further criticism, particularly from the U.S. government, it was announced that the Abe cabinet would continue to hold the Kono Statement as the Japanese government's official position. This was yet again a clear contradiction or "double talk": on the one hand Abe and his colleagues claimed they would maintain the Kono Statement as national policy, yet on the other hand they were virtually trying to defame it.

As expected, the review of the Kono Statement, which was published in June 2014, states that testimonies given by former Korean comfort women and used to draft the statement were not substantiated by other evidence, leading to the claim that they do not really verify the fact that women were forced to become sex slaves. Overall the report attempts to give the strong impression that, due to political pressure from the Korean government at the time, the Japanese government accepted those testimonies as evidence of sex slavery despite their uncertainty. In other words, it slanders former comfort women, branding them as liars. It is clear that the report was written to support the stance of the Abe cabinet by deliberately ignoring many relevant official documents that were utilized to draw up the Kono Statement. The review report is in fact a complete fabrication and a grave insult to the victims of Japan's military sex slavery.[23]

By defaming the Kono Statement in this way, the Abe cabinet invited further criticism of Abe's policy from international organizations such as the UN Human Rights Committee. In July 2014, this committee issued Concluding Observations on Japan's human rights issues, in which the way the Japanese government deals with former military sex slaves was severely condemned. It states in part: "The Committee is also concerned about re-victimization of the former comfort women by attacks on their reputations, including some by *public officials and some that are encouraged by the State party's equivocal position*"[24] (emphasis added). It is regrettable that Abe and his supporters do not realize how badly they are damaging Japan's reputation by conducting a "comfort women bashing" campaign in this way.

On August 5 and 6, 2014, *Asahi Newspaper*, a popular newspaper widely regarded as the most progressive in Japan, unexpectedly ran a series of articles on the comfort women issue. In this series, *Asahi* admitted that, among the numerous articles on the comfort women issue it has published, sixteen articles published between September 1982 and March 1997 were mistakenly based on false testimonies made by a man called Yoshida Seiji. In 1983 Yoshida published a book entitled *My War Crimes*, in which he claimed that he was responsible for abducting 205 Korean women from Jeju Island in May 1943 to make them comfort women. He received much media attention at the time and gave public talks at various places in Japan and Korea in the late 1980s and early 1990s. Not only *Asahi* but also other major Japanese newspapers, including *Sankei*, *Yomiuri*, and *Mainichi*, published articles based on Yoshida's testimony. By early 1992, however, some historians and journalists began to notice discrepancies in his talks and cast doubt on his testimony. Consequently, by the late 1990s, all the media stopped using Yoshida's testimony as a source of credible information, having noticed that Yoshida was making false testimonies to seek media attention and make money as a result.

Asahi Newspaper's sudden public admission of its mistake seventeen years after ceasing to use Yoshida's testimony is very curious. It is even stranger that *Sankei*, *Yomiuri*, and *Mainichi*, as well as a few popular weekly magazines, severely condemned *Asahi* for fabricating stories of the abductions of Korean women to make them sex slaves. They did so, pretending that they themselves had never used Yoshida's testimony in their own reportage on the comfort women issue. Several right-wing politicians took advantage of this affair, saying that the *Asahi*'s fabrication disproved testimonies by former comfort women who claimed that they had been coerced into becoming sex slaves against their will, and consequently the Kono Statement should be repudiated. Abe also criticized *Asahi*, stating that, due to its serious error, false information on comfort women had been circulated internationally with the result that many people worldwide have a completely wrong understanding of comfort women.[25] It is also strange that there were very few reports that Yoshida's testimony was never used as a source of information for producing the Kono Statement. It can only be surmised that this whole affair criticizing *Asahi* was an attempt to gain political control and to manipulate the Japanese media, the final aim being to discredit the Kono Statement yet again.

In addition to such politically motivated "comfort women bashing," racial harassment, in particular the so-called hate speech and demonstrations, against Korean residents in Japan by extremists has been increasing for several years. Despite repeated warnings on this issue by the UN Human Rights Committee, the Japanese government has not taken any serious countermeasures, stating that "freedom of speech" is guaranteed by Japan's constitution and law. Clearly, the "comfort women bashing" movement promoted by Japan's prime minister and supported by his fellow politicians and right-wing nationalists is now seriously endangering Japan's democracy.

On December 28, 2015, Japan's foreign minister Kishida Fumio and his South Korean counterpart, Yun Byung-se, made an announcement at a press conference shortly after their meeting in Seoul. They stated that Japan and South Korea have reached an agreement over the long-standing issue of comfort women, and that the Japanese government would provide ¥1 billion (US$8.3 million) to a fund to support and bankroll "projects for recovering the honor and dignity and healing the psychological wounds" of elderly former comfort women. Kishida told reporters, "Prime Minister Abe expresses anew his most sincere apologies and remorse to all the women who underwent immeasurable and painful experiences and suffered incurable physical and psychological wounds as comfort women." In return the Japanese government received assurance from the South Korean government that it would consider the matter resolved "finally and irreversibly" if Japan fulfills its promises. Yun Byung-se said that his government would also look into removing a statue symbolizing comfort women, which an activist group had erected in front of the Japanese embassy in Seoul in 2011.[26]

The "final and irreversible resolution" that the Abe cabinet requested actually meant that the Korean government should never raise the comfort women issue in any future negotiations with Japan. In other words, it meant that Abe would buy the complete silence of South Korea on the comfort women issues at the cost of ¥1 billion. The money that Japan would provide was not "compensation" because the Japanese government does not admit that it holds legal responsibility for the former comfort women. If Abe truly felt "remorse to all the women who underwent immeasurable and painful experiences and suffered incurable physical and psychological wounds as comfort women," then how could he demand the removal of a statue of comfort women, which symbolizes the deep pain suffered by victims of the Japanese military violence against women?

The day after the meeting between Kishida and Yun, Abe phoned South Korean president Park Geun-hye to repeat the apology already offered by Kishida. Yet, Abe did not express his apologies directly to the former comfort women in Korea. A few days later, the Taiwanese government issued a statement expressing its intention to seek a similar apology and financial support from the Japanese government for Taiwan's own former comfort women. Yet, the chief cabinet secretary of the Japanese government, Suga Yoshihide, quickly responded that Japan had no plan to deal with former comfort women in any nation other than Korea.[27] Furthermore, at a session of the UN Committee on the Elimination of Discrimination against Women in Geneva in February 2016, Deputy Foreign Minister Sugiyama Shinsuke yet again claimed that there was no evidence to prove that comfort women were forcefully recruited by military or government authorities, and that false reports by *Asahi* created an untruthful image of military sex slaves.[28]

In short, the comfort women issue has been highly politicized, and thus became a Japan-Korea bilateral issue in ways that neglect the "basic human rights" of the former comfort women of many different nationalities. Moreover, the Abe cabinet has no intention of changing its policies to properly address the current textbook issues and problems of history education and to firmly introduce preventative initiatives of violence against women into Japanese education and society.

Such an irresponsible and unconscionable attitude by the Japanese government has strengthened the case of former Japanese military sex slaves from Korea, Taiwan, China, the Philippines, Indonesia, and other nations, rather than silencing their voices. Their courageous acts have encouraged numerous supporters all over the world, in particular among feminist groups, including those in Japan. Without the continuous efforts of these victims to keep this issue alive and without the support of women and men from all over the world, the establishment of the International Criminal Court would not have been possible.

However, the comfort women bashing implemented by the Japanese government clearly demonstrates that military violence against women remains a fundamental concern for democracy, not just in Japan. Closely intertwined with nationalism, in particular male chauvinism and misogyny, it is a worldwide problem. Only significant reform of the culture of hegemonic masculinity and its resonance in multiple wars can rectify this situation.

NOTES

1. Most of these documents are included in Yoshimi Yoshiaki, ed., *Jugun Ianfu Shiryo-shu* (A Collection of Source Materials on Comfort Women) (Tokyo: Otsuki Shoten, 1992).

2. Ibid., doc. 34, 183–85.

3. Inaba Masao, ed., *Okamura Yasuji Taisho Shiryo* (Documents on General Okamura Yasuji), vol. l (Tokyo: Hara Shobo, 1970), 302.

4. Nankin Jiken Chosa Kenk: yu Kai, ed., *Nankin Jiken Shiryo-shu* (A Collection of Source Materials on the Nanking Incident) (Tokyo: Aoki Shoten, 1992), 211, 220, 280.

5. Kinbara Setsuzo, *Rikugun Gyomu Nisshi Tekiroku* (Army Daily Report Summary), pt. 2, September 3, 1942 (Tokyo: Japanese Defence Research Institute Archives Collection).

6. Yoshimi, *Jugun Ianfu Shiryo-shu*, docs. 67–74, 299–340.

7. Ibid., 68.

8. A summary of these fifty-one testimonies as well as the complete record of several of them are now available in Japanese. See *Firippin no Nippon-gun Ianfu: Seiteki Boryoku no Higaisha-tachi* (Filipina Comfort Women of the Japanese Military: Victims of Sexual Violence) (Tokyo: Akashi Shoten, 1995). Eighteen of these testimonies are available in English under the title "Philippine 'Comfort Women' Compensation Suit: Excerpts of the Complaint" (Task Force on Filipino Comfort Women & Japanese Committee for the Filipino Comfort Women, P.O. Box 190, 1099 Manila, the Philippines).

9. Thirty-six young Dutch women, including Jan Ruff-O'Herne, were forcibly taken from internment camps in the Dutch East Indies and put into comfort stations in Semarang in 1944. The Japanese officers who were responsible for this so-called "Semarang comfort women incident" were tried at the Batavia Temporary Court Martial in 1948. As a result, Army Major Okada was sentenced to death, and eleven others were sentenced to prison terms ranging from two to twenty years. The Japanese translation of the proceedings of this trial is available in Kajimura Taichiro, Muraoka Takamitsu, and Kasuya Koichiro, eds., *Ianfu Kyosei Renko* (The Enforced Comfort Women) (Kinyobi, Tokyo, 2008).

10. "Philippine 'Comfort Women' Compensation Suit," 17.

11. Ibid., 53.

12. Statement by the chief cabinet secretary Kono Yohei on the result of the study on the issue of comfort women (http://www.mofa.go.jp/policy/women/fund/state9308.html).

13. Ibid.

14. Tawara Yoshifumi, "Kyokasho Mondai to Uyoku no Doko" (The School Textbook Issue and the Right-Wing Movements), in Nishino Rumiko, Kim Puja, and Onozawa Akane, eds., *Ianfu Bashing o Koete: Kono Danwa to Nippon no Sekinin* (Overcome Comfort Women Bashing: The Kono Statement and Japan's Responisbility) (Otsuki Shoten, Tokyo, 2013), 162–68.

15. Tawara Yoshifumi, "Abe Shusho no Rekishi Ninshiki no Raireki o Saguru" (An Examination of the Origins of Prime Minister Abe's Historical View), in Hayashi Hirofumi, Tawara Yoshifumi, and Watanabe Mina, eds., *Murayama Kono Danwa Minaoshi no Sakkaku: Rekishi Ninshiki to Ianfu Mondai o Megutte* (Errors in the Review of the Murayama and

Kono Statements: Concerning the Historical View and the Comfort Women Issue) (Kamogawa Shoten, Kyoto, 2013), 37–63.

16. Ibid.

17. Tawara, "Kyokasho Mondai to Uyoku no Doko," in Nishino, Kim, and Onozawa, *Ianfu Bashing o Koete: Kono Danwa to Nippon no Sekinin*, 168–75.

18. Yamamoto Kentaro, "Jugun Ianfu Mondai no Keii: Kono Danwa o Meguru Ugoki o Chushin ni" (The History of the Comfort Women Issue: On Events That Occurred in Relation to the Kono Statement) (National Diet Library), September 2013 (http://dl.ndl.go.jp/view/download/digidepo_8301279_po_075204.pdf?contentNo=1).

19. Tokudome Kinue with Michael Honda, "The Japanese Apology on the 'Comfort Women' Cannot Be Considered Official: Interview with Congressman Michael Honda," in *Japan Focus* (http://japanfocus.org/-Michael-Honda/2438/article.html).

20. "Shinzo Abe's Double Talk," *Washington Post*, March 24, 2007 (http://www.washingtonpost.com/wp-dyn/content/article/2007/03/23/AR2007032301640.html).

21. "President Bush and Prime Minister Abe of Japan Participate in a Joint Press Availability," posted on White House website on April 27, 2007 (http://georgewbush-whitehouse.archives.gov/news/releases/2007/04/20070427-6.html).

22. "Text of a resolution expressing the sense of the House of Representatives that the Government of Japan should formally acknowledge, apologize, and accept historical responsibility in a clear and unequivocal manner for its Imperial Armed Forces" (https://www.govtrack.us/congress/bills/110/hres121/text).

23. Kono Danwa Sakusei Katei ni Kansuru Kento Chiimu (Examination Committee on the Process of Writing the Kono Statement), *Ianfu Mondai o Meguru Nikkan-kan no Yaritori no Keii: Kono Danwa Sakusei kara Ajia Josei Kikin made* (The Negotiations between Japan and Korea on the Comfort Women Issue: From the Kono Statement to Asian Women's Fund) (Cabinet Secretariat Office), June 20, 2014 (http://www.kantei.go.jp/jp/kakugikettei/2014/__icsFiles/afieldfile/2014/06/20/20140620houkokusho_2.pdf).

24. UN Human Rights Committee, Concluding Observations on the Sixth Periodic Report of Japan (http://tbinternet.ohchr.org/Treaties/

CERD/Shared%20Documents/JPN/CERD_C_JPN_CO_7-9_18106_E.
pdf).

25. "Ianfu Mondai de Nippon Kizutsuketa Shusho Asahi Shimbun ni
taishi" (Prime Minister Criticized the *Asahi Newspaper*'s Report on
Comfort Women Damaged Japan), *Asahi Newspaper*, September 12,
2014.

26. "Japan and South Korea Agree WW2 'Comfort Women' Deal,"
BBC, December 28, 2015 (http://www.bbc.com/news/world-asia-
35188135).

27. "Suga Rules Out Taiwan Talks, Says Japan's 'Comfort Women'
Deal Applies Only to South Korea," *Japan Times*, January 5, 2016.

28. "No Documents Confirm Military Coerced 'Comfort Women,' Japan Envoy Tells U.N.," *Japan Times*, February 17, 2016.

I

MY MOTHER, JULIA

My story begins in the barrio of Pampang, in Angeles, Pampanga, about eighty kilometers north of Manila. My grandfather, Alberto Luna, lived in that barrio. He was a farmer in a sugarcane and rice plantation owned by a rich landlord named Don Pepe Henson.

At that time, farmers in Pampanga were very poor. They got only one-third of the rice they harvested and a meager daily wage for the sugarcane that they cut or planted. Alberto's father had been a farmer, too, and Alberto inherited the work in the plantation when his father died. My grandfather plowed the ricefields with his carabao in May, when the first rains began. He harvested in December, when the *palay* was ripe. After the harvest, he plowed the fields again to plant sugarcane, which was ready for cutting and milling by the time the rainy season began. It was an endless cycle of hard work from which my father and my grandfather did not escape. They were always in debt, and they lived and died in poverty.

Alberto started courting my grandmother, Carmen Salas, when she was only fifteen. Carmen had other suitors, including an American soldier who wanted to marry her. Her family were farmers, too, but she helped her aunts sell fruits to American soldiers stationed in Fort Stotsenburg, which later became Clark Air Base. They peddled bananas, *chico*, mangoes and other fruits which they loaded on a cart pulled by a carabao. That was how Carmen met American soldiers. That was also how she learned to speak English fluently.

Carmen's parents did not like the soldiers. They agreed with Alberto's parents that he and Carmen should be married. For one year, as was the custom then, Alberto put himself at the service of Carmen's parents. He fetched water for the household, helped Carmen's father in the fields, chopped wood in the forest for cooking.

After long months of proving the sincerity of his intentions through hard work, Alberto married Carmen in a church ceremony. Within a year, my mother Julia was born, and after her came nine more children.

The couple had a hard time raising their children because they were very poor. While Alberto was in the fields, Carmen stayed home to do the chores. Sometimes their relatives helped them meet their needs. Everyone in the barrio helped each other. That was the tradition, and even now, this tradition exists.

My mother was born on April 15, 1907. It was she who told me the story of her childhood and my birth.

My mother said that one day in 1920, when she was thirteen, Don Pepe Henson visited the barrio as he usually did every afternoon. As he was walking around our village, it suddenly rained very hard. Don Pepe sought shelter in my grandfather's hut. He was surprised to see Alberto, Carmen and their five children huddled in one corner of the house. Their cogon roof was leaking, and the entire family was taking shelter in the only dry spot in the hut.

When he saw Don Pepe, Alberto stood up and kissed his hand in respect. He offered the landlord his *salakot*, so he would not get wet. When the rain stopped, Don Pepe spoke to my grandfather. "Alberto," he said, "it is better to make do with only two meals daily as long as your house does not get wet when it rains. This is very bad for your small children." Alberto was so shamed he could not say anything. He only bowed his head. He was so poor, he could not even afford to have his roof repaired.

Suddenly Julia came in. She was very cold and wet. She had been sent on an errand to the neighbor's to borrow a *ganta* of rice, because the family had no rice for dinner. Don Pepe saw her. "So you have a bigger daughter," he told Alberto. "How old is she?"

"She is thirteen years old, sir," said Carmen.

Don Pepe then asked the couple whether they would allow their daughter to work as a maid in his house. "Just for me and my wife, because my children have their own maids," the landlord added.

"Sir, Carmen and I will discuss the matter," Alberto replied. Don Pepe nodded and told them he wanted an answer within a week. Then he left and inspected the roofs of the other houses in the village to see whether they were leaking, too. The landlord advanced the money for repairs, and the tenants paid him during the harvest season when they got their share of the crop.

Alberto and Carmen stayed up late that night talking about the landlord's request. The next day, they told Julia what Don Pepe wanted. She understood that her parents wanted her to work for the landowner. She felt sad because she would have to move to the big house and would no longer see her playmates and her cousins. She would especially miss her cousin Anna, who was a year older and with whom she was really close, and her friends Rita and Alfonso.

Three days later, Don Pepe returned to Alberto's house. He wanted to know the couple's response. Alberto and Carmen said yes, Julia was willing to be the landlord's maid. They had no choice. They thought that if they disagreed, Don Pepe might not allow Alberto to work in the farm. And where would they go if that happened?

The landlord told Alberto to take Julia to his house the next day. The following morning, Alberto got up early, yoked his carabao and cart to take some firewood for the landlord, and delivered Julia to the big house, which still exists today. Don Pepe and his wife invited Alberto and Julia to the huge *sala* with antique chairs and chandeliers lit with candles. Julia was astonished, because she had never seen a living room as spacious and a house as beautiful.

The landlord gave Alberto some money as advance payment for Julia's work. She was to get five pesos every month as salary and some old clothes. Alberto got an advance of one hundred twenty pesos, his daughter's wages for two years, and left. Julia sobbed quietly as she watched her father depart.

Doña Saring, Don Pepe's wife, taught Julia what to do in the house. Julia learned easily and did her work well. The doña was very happy with Julia because she was an obedient maid. But my mother was homesick; she often thought of her own mother and her brothers and sisters.

Every week, Julia saw her father who would come to the big house to bring firewood, vegetables and fresh carabao's milk for the landlord. With the money from Julia's wages, her family was able to repair their house and replace their leaking thatched roof with an iron one.

After two years, Julia blossomed into a beautiful young woman. One day, she visited her family in the barrio. Her brothers and sisters did not recognize her because they were too young when she left. She stayed with her parents for one week, helping her mother who had just given birth to the family's seventh child. Julia was happy to see her childhood friends again. Her friends were young men and women now, too.

Every night, the young men serenaded her. They waited outside her window, strumming their guitars and singing love songs. Alberto usually invited them in. They sat in the living room, talking and singing. Julia sang, too. Then she served them hot *salabat* and boiled *kamote*.

The next week, Julia returned to her work as a maid in the big house. This time, even the landlord's children began to take notice of her. Don Pepe had ten children, all of whom were already grown up. The second to the youngest daughter was Julia's age.

Don Pepe was a very religious man, and his wife was a kind woman who treated Julia well. Twice everyday, at six in the morning and again at dusk, the landlord and his wife went to the old church in Angeles to pray and hear mass. Their children were also

Don Pepe, our landlord and my father.

very religious. In every corner of the big house there were statues of the Virgin Mary, Jesus Christ and the saints.

One night, while Julia was fast asleep, she felt someone kiss her. She wanted to scream, but she heard a voice whispering in her ear, "Do not shout, nobody can hear you because only my wife and I are in the house. All my children are not here." Julia was scared, she could not fight back because Don Pepe was stronger than she was. He raped her. Julia felt great pain. When he was through, he told her not to tell her parents about the incident. "Or

Alberto, my grandfather, returning home with his carabao and slide cart after delivering food and firewood to the "big house."

else, I will kick out your father from my land," he said. Then he walked away from Julia's room.

My mother was then only fifteen years old and had just begun to have her period. The next morning, she did her work obediently. She set the table for breakfast and served the landlord and his wife their meal. Don Pepe glanced at Julia very often. She kept quiet, but in her heart she was very angry.

One day, Julia asked the landlord's wife for permission to visit her parents. She went to the barrio and stayed two days with her family. Her mother and her brothers and sisters were happy to see her. Before she left, she talked to her parents and told them what had happened. But her parents refused to believe her. "Don Pepe is a religious man, he will not do that," her father said. But Alberto knew in his heart that she was telling the truth. Julia did not know till later that her father was bitter and angry, too. This is happening to us because we are poor, he thought.

Julia cried. Maybe my parents don't love me anymore, she sobbed. She left the house weeping, and desperate about her situation. She wanted to run away somewhere, anywhere. She did not want to go back to the big house. But she was afraid. She could neither read nor write. Her parents did not send her to school because she had to take care of her baby sister and brothers.

So Julia returned to the landlord's house and worked as usual, her heart full of anger and resentment.

This story comes from my mother's own lips. She told me all that happened to her before I was born. She told me not only once but many times. That is why this is written in the diary of my mind.

From the day Julia confessed what had been done to her, Alberto was never the same again. Carmen noticed Alberto was always sad and she understood that it was because of Julia. She, too, felt Julia's pain.

One day Alberto became very sick. He refused to eat and was always in deep thought. He was sometimes in tears. Carmen tried to comfort her husband. "What can I do for you, Alberto?" she said. "We have no money to see a doctor."

Alberto only smiled bitterly and said, "It's not getting worse; it's just a slight fever."

Carmen could feel all the pain and bitterness in her husband's heart. Before long, his fever got worse, and he found it difficult to breathe. One day, the landlord visited them and saw Alberto in a bad state.

He asked Carmen to take her husband to the town hospital. He also gave Carmen some money. Alberto was confined for two weeks. The doctor said that he had pneumonia, and that was the reason for the high fever and difficult breathing.

When Alberto was well and ready to return home, the doctor instructed him not to work in the fields again. He was told to rest at home. Without an income, his family survived only because the landlord supported them.

Julia was still working in the big house, not knowing her father was sick. She found out only when one of her relatives went to the landlord's house and told her. That same afternoon, Julia asked Doña Saring for permission to visit her father.

Julia was happy to be home, she even forgot her sadness for a while. She met her childhood friends, especially Anna, her cousin and close friend. She and Anna chatted, laughing and recollecting the times when they were young children.

Anna had grown into a beautiful woman. When they were talking intimately, Anna whispered, "Julia, I want you to be my maid of honor, because I will be marrying an American soldier at Fort Stotsenburg."

"You're joking," said Julia.

"It is true, my parents have given their permission. His name is William. He wants the wedding to be held at the camp, but my parents want it in the Catholic church of Angeles," said Anna. "I will ask your mother if she will let you."

Julia only smiled. "Do you love him?" she asked.

"Oh yes, I love him very much, and he, too, loves me very much," Anna replied.

When Anna left, there was a great sadness in Julia's heart.

Rita also came to visit and chat about friends. She mentioned Alfonso, her brother. "He wants to see you, too," Rita said. One night, Alfonso and his male friends serenaded Julia. He returned every Saturday night to visit and court her.

Julia was very disturbed because she knew that she was not a virgin anymore. She did not know whether she should encourage Alfonso's visits.

When she saw her father, Julia cried. Her mother was crying, too, saying that due to his illness, Alberto could not work in the farm anymore. For the first time, Julia learned that it was Don Pepe who was providing for her family's daily needs.

It dawned on Julia that she could not run away from the landlord's shadow. She cried secretly when she remembered Don Pepe's cruelty. She could not protest against his advances anymore. She realized that were it not for his money, her father might have died. And the financial support Don Pepe gave her family kept them alive. Her salary was too small to feed six brothers and sisters.

Julia did not want to go back to work in the big house. But Carmen told her she should because the landlord might be angry and call them ungrateful.

Julia obeyed her mother. For the next three years, Julia worked in the big house. Don Pepe did not touch her again, until one night when he crawled into her room and raped her one more time. Julia could not fight back; neither could she tell anyone of the incident. Then, not long afterward, the landlord raped her again.

Finally, Don Pepe himself visited Alberto and Carmen to confess the things that he had done to Julia. "I fell in love with your daughter, that is why I dared to do that," Don Pepe said. He added that he wanted to keep seeing Julia. "Do not worry too much, I promise I will support you and your family."

Two months later, Don Pepe sent Julia back home, for fear that she would tell his wife about what he did to her. Julia did not know that he had spoken to her parents. While at home, she was happy and forgot her pain for a while.

She spent a lot of time with her childhood friends. When the moon was full, they played hide and seek and sang songs until they were sleepy. On Saturday nights, Julia received men of her age who courted her. But she felt shame because she had lost her virginity. At that time, a woman considered her virginity the most valuable gift she could give her husband-to-be.

One day, Carmen told Julia to stop admitting suitors. Don Pepe has talked with your father about his plan to get in touch with you, she said. He will provide for our financial needs if we will agree to let you live with him, said Carmen.

Julia was very surprised. "Why, I do not love that old man. He is older than my grandfather," she said.

Carmen slapped her. "Obey what we want you to do. We are grateful because he helped us when your father was sick. And without him, we will have nothing to eat."

Julia ran to her room and wept. She cried and cried until she fell asleep. When dinner time came, she refused to leave her room. Carmen went to her and called out in a soft voice. She comforted Julia and apologized for slapping her. "You know your father also agrees that we should give in to the landlord's plea," she explained. "He promised to give us all the things that we need." But Julia just kept quiet.

She also refused to eat. She stayed in her room for three days. When Carmen returned, she addressed her daughter in an angry tone. "If you refuse what the landlord wants, then go and pay all our debts and give us the benefits that the landlord is giving us now. Otherwise, your father and I will despise you. You are not a good daughter. You are selfish." Then Carmen stormed out of the room, very angry.

My mother was then nineteen years old. She was deeply hurt. Tears gushed from her eyes. She did not want to hurt her mother. Julia was a very obedient daughter. So she followed her angry mother and spoke to her.

"I will not protest anymore, Mother," she said, fighting back tears.

Carmen smiled and said in a low voice, "It is for your own good, Julia."

At that time, Julia was already feeling awful things inside her body. Her period had been delayed for two months. When she told her mother, Carmen was happy, because a baby meant that the landlord would remain their benefactor for a long time. Alberto was glad, too.

Don Pepe came every day to see Julia. One day, he asked her parents for permission to take her away with him for a while. He instructed Carmen to escort her to a hotel in a nearby town.

Julia did just as her mother told her. For two days, she was with the landlord in the hotel. She did not love him and hated having sex with him. When Don Pepe left, Carmen came to the hotel to fetch her.

Twice a month, until the fifth month of her pregnancy, Julia was taken to the hotel for her date with the landlord. Every day the landlord came to visit her. The neighbors were beginning to wonder why the landlord was at their home so often.

Don Pepe decided to take Julia and her family somewhere else because he wanted to hide from the village what he had done. He was known to be a very religious man and was respected by many because he was a big landowner. He discussed the matter with Julia's parents.

Carmen remembered she had a niece living in Pasay, about three kilometers from Manila. She paid her niece a visit and told her about Julia and the landlord. Carmen found a house for rent only a block from where her niece lived.

The landlord gave Carmen and Alberto money to move their entire family to Pasay. They went on board a train, Alberto and Carmen and their children, Julia among them. At that time, Carmen had just given birth to her tenth child. In the seven years that had passed since Julia first went to work for the landlord, Carmen had three more children.

2

MY CHILDHOOD

I was born on December 5, 1927. A midwife attended to my delivery at home. My mother had a difficult time. The pain of childbirth combined with the sadness in her heart. She was having the child of a man she did not love. But when Julia offered her breast to her infant, she was filled with happiness. She said to herself, "Thank God, I have overcome the hard times and the pain of giving birth to this beautiful and healthy child."

About a month after I was born, Carmen visited the landlord to give Don Pepe the news. He had not seen Julia since her family moved to Pasay. The landlord wrote out a name on a piece of paper. It was "Maria Rosa Luna Henson." That was the name he gave me, and he instructed my grandmother to register it in the Pasay municipal hall.

After six months, Don Pepe went to Pasay. He greeted Julia and held and kissed her baby. Julia's eyes were gloomy because she felt no love for him. But Don Pepe was happy. By the time I was born he was fifty-six years old, and my mother had just turned twenty.

Julia passed the days looking after her baby. She was happy taking care of the infant. But she was under her mother's control. Carmen held the money that the landlord gave. Julia never learned how to count, so she was not entrusted with her own money. Carmen just gave her a few pesos and bought clothes for her and her baby. Carmen directed her life. Sometimes my mother worried, what would happen to her and her child if the landlord died?

I saw my father for the first time when I was three years old. I did not want to approach him, but he was very happy to see me because I looked very much like him. Every two months, my mother, grandmother and I went to see my father at the Escolta, which was then Manila's business district. My father owned a pharmacy there. He met us in a restaurant, and he talked to my mother while we ate.

He continued to support not only my mother and me but also Carmen's entire family. Julia's brothers and sisters all depended on Don Pepe's money, whether they lived in the house in Pasay, or in their own houses after they got married. None of them had a job. They became even more dependent on Don Pepe after my grandfather died when I was five years old. At one time, five of my mother's relatives from Pampanga stayed in the house in Pasay for almost two months. All of them were fed with Don Pepe's money. Julia resented this. How could she save any money for her and her child if everyone depended on her?

Three of my mother's sisters, Aniceta, Laria and Consing, and her brother Ando married while they were still in their teens. All of them managed to attend school, but stopped after the second grade after they had learned to read and write. The landlord's money paid for the tuition of Julia's brothers, Juan, Pedro, Felino and Emil, in a private school in Pasay.

For years, all of them depended on Don Pepe's support. Even though Julia's married sisters and brother no longer lived in the house in Pasay, they went to visit Julia every month to ask for some money and food. Pedro later worked in Don Pepe's house.

The day came when the monthly support from the landlord was no longer sufficient. By that time, I was seven years old and needed to go to school. Don Pepe had instructed my mother to take care of my education.

I was enrolled in a Catholic school run by nuns, St. Mary's Academy. I was very bright in class. Although my father gave extra money for my studies, I was always short of the things we needed in school. Sometimes I had no writing pad or pencils. I had only two uniforms.

But my teachers were very good to me. I also had many friends. I was very good in all my subjects. I learned fast and did well even in handicraft, embroidery, sewing and knitting.

One day, Don Pepe asked me about my studies. I told him how difficult our life was. "My mother and I are very poor," I said, "because my grandmother does not give us money and there is no money for my schooling."

I asked my father many questions. I told him my classmates were always asking why he never attended the parents' meeting. And why did he give me two names?

"Because you were born on December 5, 1927," he said. "The day was Monday, so I gave you the name Rosa, which means rose. Do you know what is celebrated on the first Monday of December?"

"Yes," I answered. "That's Mother's Day. You're supposed to pin a red rose on the left side of your chest if your mother is still alive, a white rose if you have no more mother."

My father smiled happily. "I gave you the name Maria because Maria is a popular name for Catholic girls like you."

Then I asked, "Why are you not living with us? Do you work far away?"

He was quiet. "Ask your mother about this matter," he said. "She can explain all these things."

I learned later that my father had his own family. My mother told me the things that happened in her life. I pitied her very much, especially because she could neither write nor read. She did not even know how to count. I worried about her. I studied very hard because she was illiterate. My dream was to redeem her sad life.

I envied my classmates and friends who were with their fathers during class meetings. One day my teacher invited me to have lunch with her. As we were eating, the teacher asked, "Rosa, is your father still alive?"

"Still alive," I said. "But he has his own family. He is not living with my mother." I answered truthfully, even if I knew that an illegitimate child is not treated well.

I don't think that my teacher was very talkative. But later on other teachers began to know about me. And some of my classmates began teasing me. "You are like wild grass," one of them said. "You just sprouted from the soil."

My friends and classmates heard her. But I only laughed and recited a stanza from a poem we had learned in school:

"All things bright and beautiful,
All creatures great and small,
All things wise and wonderful,
The Lord God made them all."

They all fell quiet. Maybe they were embarrassed. So I just went on reciting, on the verge of tears:

"Each little flower that opens,
Each little bird that sings,
He made their glowing colors,
He made their tiny wings."

Then the tears started flowing down my cheeks. I cannot describe what I felt. My classmates cried, too. "Rosa, we are very sorry to hurt you," one of them said. "You have a big heart . . . You are still our best friend."

I only sobbed, because I pitied myself. It was not my fault that my mother bore me out of wedlock. But I thought it would have been worse if my mother had aborted me. I was her only happiness. Without me, she would have gone crazy, thinking that her life was meaningless.

I tried to study harder still, so I could get higher grades. I was the brightest pupil in my class. I got high marks in all my subjects. I wanted to become a doctor someday.

One day as I passed a crowd of students, one of them said, "You are not qualified to study in this Catholic school because you are an illegitimate child."

"As long as the superiors of this school allow me to study here, and as long as I can pay the tuition, no one can stop me from attending classes," I answered angrily.

"Who are you?" I asked. "Are you a saint from above who has come down to judge me?" The student did not say a single word. All the other students were frightened. They didn't expect that I could growl at them like a tiger.

I wanted to be humble and did not want to argue with those who wanted to hurt me. But I could not endure the taunts. The truth was that I loved my father, and I was always eager to embrace him and to talk with him even though I knew all about his own family.

Maybe God intends something for me, I thought. There must be a reason why he created me this way, an illegitimate child. I comforted myself with these thoughts and tried to drive away my loneliness.

One time, I insisted on visiting Don Pepe's house. I asked my grandmother to take me to Angeles, Pampanga. She agreed, and I was very happy and excited that I could embrace my father soon.

We took a train. The trip to Angeles lasted three hours. I was very anxious to see the house where my father lived and where my mother once worked. When we got to the house, my grandmother told me that I could not go inside the house.

"I will leave you here and call your father. Just wait for me here," she said. She left me near a very big rice granary behind the big house, which was just at the back of the Catholic church. Then after thirty minutes, my grandmother came back and told me to go inside the rice granary.

I saw my father there. It was a warehouse full of sacks of rice. I paid him my respects by kissing his hand. "Oh, father, I am very eager to see you," I said. "I also want to see your children and visit

your big house." Don Pepe had eleven children with his legal wife.
His ninth child was the same age as my mother.

My father looked at me with doubt on his face. "I cannot allow
you to go in my house because my children will see you and they
do not know you," he said. He also asked me about my mother.

"Please, Father," I asked, "let me see you every month, even
only in this terrible place." He was quiet. "I see that you are
ashamed of me," I said.

I saw his face turn red, maybe from anger at the harsh words he
had heard from me. He asked me about my studies. I answered
him politely, not telling him how difficult my mother's situation
was under my grandmother's command. "I gave the money to your
grandmother," he said. Then he kissed me and handed me a small
piece of paper.

When he left, I went to my grandmother who was waiting for
me beside the church. I read the piece of paper to her. "After two
months, I will see you again in this place at ten a.m." The date and
the day were typed with the message.

While my grandmother and I were walking to the train station,
I asked her, "How did my father type these words before he came
to see me? You stayed in his house only for thirty minutes."

"The last month that I came here, I said to your father that I
will take you to see him," she said. "Maybe he typed that message
even before you arrived."

When we reached home, I told my mother that Don Pepe had
asked how she was. Then I realized why the message was typed.
He did not want anything in his own handwriting that would serve
as evidence that he acknowledged me as his illegitimate daughter.
Maybe he thought that someday I would sue him. I was angry with
him because he was ashamed of me.

After two months, I again went with my grandmother to Angeles. I went straight to the rice granary to wait for my father.
There was a narrow path near the granary, and I sat on a piece of
rock that lay on the path.

There were people passing by, and they all looked at me. Then
I saw Don Pepe's daughter on her way to church. She saw me, too,

and looked at me from head to toe. I knew immediately that she was my father's daughter because we looked alike.

I waited for more than an hour for my father. I felt like a thief hiding near the granary. When at last my father came, I went inside.

"Father, when can I see you publicly?" I asked. "I do not like this situation, it's as if I were hunting for prey. I want to see your big house, your wife and children, too."

"I will not allow you to see me anymore if you do not stop asking so many questions," he said. I saw that he was irked with me. "Be a good girl and obey me. The day will come when all of your wishes will come true."

He handed me a typewritten piece of paper and a sealed envelope with money. "Give this envelope to your grandma," he said.

I looked at my father before I left. He looked very sad and lonely. I pitied him. He seemed very old. He was sixty-nine by then. When my grandmother saw me, she asked me for the envelope. I gave it to her but she did not open it, so I never knew how much money my father was giving.

We visited the barrio where my grandmother's relatives lived. They were very happy to see me. I felt close to them because during Christmas, fiestas and school vacations, my mother and I would visit them. All of them knew I was Don Pepe's daughter.

The next day we returned home to Pasay, and I shared with my mother my conversation with my father.

One day my grandmother became ill, and she told my mother that she wanted to return to Angeles. Two months later, she died of stomach ulcers. Don Pepe gave money for burial expenses. I was then thirteen years old.

With my grandmother gone, my mother's brother Juan sometimes went to my father to get the money for us.

My childhood memories are painful. We lived in poverty even if I was a landlord's daughter. I was bitter about my mother's situation. I resented my grandmother's greed. She did not even give my mother a chance to be happy.

I loved my mother very much. I loved my father, too, because he gave me his name even though I was an illegitimate child. But he was ashamed of me, especially because he was known to be a devout man.

His wife did not know about me. My mother herself was very ashamed to show her face to Doña Saring, who had been very kind to her and treated her as one of her children when she was working in their house as a maid.

As a young girl, I earned money by teaching my classmates embroidery and knitting. During the break, I sat down with them, and they paid me three to five centavos for each kind of stitch that I taught them. I used the money to buy some thread and cloth to make handkerchiefs.

On Saturdays and Sundays, I worked with our neighbor who was a dressmaker. I hemmed the dresses and sewed on the buttons and clasps and got paid five centavos for every dress I finished. I did about five dresses in a day and saved the money to buy things I needed in school.

I enjoyed sewing. I loved to watch our neighbor make dresses. Later she showed me how to cut dresses and sew them. Until now, I like to sew and make dresses. But my childhood dream was to become a doctor. I had hoped that my father could afford to pay for my studies. I worked hard in school and aimed to become the class valedictorian when I graduated.

My dream to become a doctor began when I was in the fourth grade. I was inspired by our family doctor whose daughter, Lourdes, went to the same school as I. The doctor knew that I was the illegitimate daughter of a landlord. He also he knew that I was one of the brightest in my class.

One day the doctor asked me, "What do you like to be when you finish high school?"

"I want to be a doctor, like you," I answered.

"Why?" he asked.

"Because I want to treat my mother, my relatives and other people," I said.

My Catholic-school uniform. As a young girl I dreamed of becoming a doctor.

"You can attain your dream because you are a bright student," he said, looking at his daughter. Lourdes smiled and said, "My father knows because I told him that you are more intelligent than I."

That made me study even harder. Some of my schoolmates were envious of me. But I had good friends, too, Virginia and

Estela, who both belonged to rich families. Sometimes they asked me to help them with their homework. They were both very polite and nice to me. I helped them during the break, when we ate our sandwiches. We wrote paragraphs together or memorized stanzas of poems.

In school, we learned about the lives of saints and were taught all kinds of prayers. Every Sunday, we went to Mass and fasted during Holy Week.

At home, I played with our neighbors' children. But I had only half an hour to play because I had to do errands for my mother, who tried to make extra money by selling rice cakes and *biko*, a desert made from sticky rice, brown sugar and coconut milk. Even after both her parents had died, my mother continued supporting her brothers and sisters. The money my father gave us was never enough for all the mouths that had to be fed.

From my childhood, my mother told me the story of her life. "If I did not have you, Rosa," she used to tell me, "I would have gone mad, because my parents and the landlord ruined all my life's hopes. I may be illiterate, but I should have been given the right to choose what I want for my life."

"But I have no regrets," she continued, "because of you, Rosa, and also my brothers and sisters who benefited from the landlord." My mother always cried when she told me this. I felt great pity for her. I would whisper to myself, "I will study better so that I can fulfill my dream to become a doctor. My mother did not study because her parents did not let her. But I have this chance to study well."

My mother and I would hug each other and cry. I could see how she lived in misery because she was an obedient daughter. She feared her mother. When Carmen raised her voice, Julia cowered.

"I promise, Rosa, that I will not treat you that way. I will not do to you what my parents do to me," my mother said. "I became strong and happy only because of you."

3

THE WAR BEGINS

I celebrated my fourteenth birthday on December 5, 1941. It was a Friday. My mother cooked special food—noodles, *leche flan* and *menudo*—to mark the day. We had the meal with *calamansi* juice cooled with ice. Three of my classmates were there, as were my uncles and aunts and some neighbors. Three days later, Pearl Harbor was bombed by Japanese troops. The Second World War had begun.

On December 8, 1941, a Monday, I went to school as usual. I was in the seventh grade and would have gone on to high school in a few months. When I reached the school, I was surprised to see so many students outside the gate. The nuns had just announced that the school was closed because war had been declared. So I walked back to our house, which was about half a kilometer away.

I saw many people walking to and fro, not knowing what to do now that war had erupted.

The next morning, my mother, our relatives and our neighbor evacuated to a village near Ipo Dam in Bulacan. The following day, December 10, Japanese troops landed in Luzon.

We fled to Bulacan because my uncle was a truck driver who worked in a cement quarry near the dam. He took all of us, with all our belongings, on board his truck. As we were driving out of Manila, I thought of my father. I saw the other children who had their fathers with them. I wondered whether my father was also evacuating like we were. Was he with his wife and children? My father was very old, seventy-two when the war broke out.

Like me, my mother was very scared. But she told me not to bother myself with worries about my father. We spent the next month in the barrio of Bigte in Norzagaray, Bulacan. We lived in a cave which was so huge it was like a church. It was made of white rock which shone like marble.

We stayed there about a month with several families, including my uncles Juan, Emil, Felino and Ando, who brought his wife and children; my aunts Consing, who was single, and Laria, whose husband drove the truck. Several of our neighbors were there with us, too. We survived by helping the village folk nearby plant rice and harvest vegetables. The men went to the dam to fish. We washed our clothes in the river and cooked our meals out in the sun.

After a while, two of my uncles, Juan and Ando, decided to go to my father's house not only to see how he was doing, but also to find out about another uncle, Pedro, who was then eighteen years old. Pedro had been instructed to work in the big house so that my father and I could remain in touch after my grandmother's death.

My two uncles walked all of fifty kilometers from Norzagaray to Angeles. It took them four days to reach my father's house. Don Pepe gave my uncle Juan some money. He said that my mother and I should be careful because the Japanese Imperial Army might land in Lingayen, Pangasinan, and would be in our area soon.

My uncles walked back to where we were and reached our evacuation site just before Christmas of 1941. They gave us the money my father sent and told us that my uncle Pedro was alright. I felt I was very lucky to have a thoughtful father who knew I needed his support in such difficult times. I thought it was better to have a supportive father, even though I was an illegitimate child, than a father who abandoned his family and ran away when they needed him. That is why I loved my father very much.

We spent Christmas and New Year in the cave. [...]
cold. The place was swarming with mosquitoes, and [...]
fires so the smoke would drive the insects away. We v[...]
mood to celebrate. We had our usual meal and then went to sleep.

I saw Japanese soldiers for the first time about a week later. The first glimpse I had of them was of twenty armed soldiers riding bicycles. Behind them, scores more marched in formation. We were in the village harvesting rice when they passed us. We hid ourselves behind tall cogon grasses and watched them march. Then we ran back to the cave.

On December 26,1941, Gen. Douglas MacArthur, commander of the United States Armed Forces in the Far East (Usaffe), proclaimed Manila an "open city." Guns were withdrawn from the capital in compliance with international law. When we heard the announcement, we decided it was safe to return to our home in Pasay. Besides, we feared that we would all fall ill in the mosquito-infested cave. We went on foot, walking through the mountains to our home. It was a very difficult route, and we were very afraid that we might encounter the Japanese Army. We rested in the houses of peasants in the mountains who shared their food with us.

Japanese troops occupied Manila in early January 1942. Life in the city was difficult. Food and money were hard to come by. My uncles and our neighbor decided to make extra money by getting firewood from Fort McKinley, a huge American military reservation near our area which had been taken over by the Japanese. The fort was about an hour's walk from where we lived. My uncles chopped the wood into pieces, bundled them and sold them for fuel. One day I asked my mother if I could join my uncles and fetch firewood for our own use. My mother refused at first, but I kept asking her. In the end, she allowed me to go.

For one week, I went every day with my uncles to gather wood. I was happy to have fuel for cooking even though I got ant bites and bruises from walking past thorny trees and grass.

One day in February 1942, at about eleven a.m., as I was preparing to bundle some dry branches that I had gathered, I was surprised by two Japanese soldiers who grabbed each of my arms. I cried out, but they refused to let me go. Then I heard someone shout, "*Baka!*" I thought the word meant cow, because *baka* is the Tagalog word for cow. It was only later that I found out it was a Japanese swearword that meant stupid. The shout came from another Japanese soldier who approached us and slapped the two soldiers who held me. He looked like an officer because he carried a long, curved saber. I thought he would save me, but he grabbed me from the soldiers and raped me.

When he was done, he passed me on to the two soldiers, who took turns raping me. Then they just walked away. It was a very painful experience. My genitals bled and ached so much. I could not even stand. Luckily, a farmer passed by and took me to his hut. His wife gave me a dress because my skirt was full of blood, and I could not hide what had happened to me. I stayed with them for two days, and then I walked back, following the train tracks to our house. My uncles were still looking for me, thinking I had gotten lost.

Assaulted by the Japanese. The officer with the saber, who was the first to rape me, I later learned was Captain Tanaka.

I told my mother what had happened to me. She cried and told me I was still lucky because they did not kill me. She advised me not to talk about the incident to anybody. But I was very sad. I could feel the pain inside me. I was fourteen, and had not yet begun to menstruate. I kept thinking, why did this happen to me? I remembered the landlord who had raped my mother.

Did I inherit my mother's fate?

I rested at home for about two weeks. Without my mother's permission, I again joined my neighbors and my uncles in gathering wood. "I will not get out of the sight of my uncles and neighbors," I told myself. But as we reached the place where we usually went, we saw Japanese soldiers. One of them was the same officer who had raped me.

He grabbed me in full view of my uncles and neighbors. They could not do anything because they could get killed. My uncles just cried because they could not help me. After raping me, the officer just walked away.

How was it possible to have the misfortune of being sexually abused again? When my mother learned that I was raped again, she decided to take me to her hometown. It was the last day of March 1942.

We lived in Pampang, my grandfather's barrio on the outskirts of Angeles. Our house was in the middle of a forest. It was a small hut made of bamboo and had a roof of cogon grass. We stayed there with my uncles and other relatives.

The house was owned by my mother's cousin. He was known as Kumander Pinatubo and was a leader of the Hukbalahap, the Filipino people's army resisting Japanese invaders. There were many Huk meetings held in his house. One day he asked me if I wanted to be a member of the Huk. I said yes because I was angry after what had happened to me. But I did not tell anybody that I had been raped. Only my mother and my uncles knew.

The organization assigned me to collect food, medicine and clothes for the guerrillas.

Many of the townsfolk helped and gave their support. Mine was a dangerous mission because there were so many pro-Japanese spies, Filipinos who belonged to the dreaded Makapili.

Once a month there was a Huk meeting which was held sometimes in our house, sometimes in another place. I met many members of the organization, mostly men and a few women. Their ages ranged from eighteen to forty-five. Many of them had guns, but I did not hold a gun nor become a combatant. Once a month I collected some medicine from Huk sympathizers, some of whom were drugstore owners. My father contributed. He owned a pharmacy in Angeles, and he knew that I was with the Hukbalahap.

Sometimes I saw his children, but they never acknowledged that I was their half-sister.

Despite my resemblance to Don Pepe, they refused to believe that their father could have an illegitimate daughter. They were part of a rich and famous family in our town. They were very proud of their father and did not want his reputation damaged. They probably also thought I might claim a share of their inheritance.

A Hukbalahap meeting.

But I did not let their attitude worry me. The happiest moments in my life were when I was with the Hukbalahap, collecting the medicine that I knew would be a big help to the guerrillas. There were many who joined the Huk. I was not the youngest participant. Boys as young as seven to ten years old served as couriers for the organization. They were brave. I also befriended the guerrillas who came to our house and some of the women combatants whom I saw during meetings. They initiated encounters with Japanese soldiers in order to seize guns and ammunition.

The Hukbalahap had a song which I can still sing today. Its lyrics are in Pampango:

> *Pamisan metung a panig mitatag ya*
> *Lalam nang bandila ning balen tang sinta*
> *Bang mayatbus lubus ing katimawan na*
> *Ning panga bansang Pilipinas.*
>
> *Lalaki't babai, matua't kayanakan*
> *Misan metung tamo king pamakilaban*
> *Harapan ta lang Hapones a yalung paylakuan*
> *Lalo na itang kayanakan,*
>
> *Dapat lang itabi ding pasistang Hapones*
> *A berdugo ning lahi*
> *Kinamkam king pibandian*
> *Lepastangan do puri deting babai*
>
> *Viva Hukbalahap! makanian tang igulisak*
>
> *King puri nang mesintang ning balen tang meduhagi.*
> *Dakal lang taong mengayalang kalma*
> *Karing penabtab da batal*
> *Kaybat depatan ngara e tala kalaban*
> *Hiling kabalat tula naman.*

(Once a group was formed
Beneath the banner of our beloved land
To free from slavery
The Philippines, our country.

Men and women,
Young and old,
Let us join together
To fight the Japanese.

We must vanquish the fascist Japanese,
The scourge of our race.
They seized all our wealth,
Raped our women and killed our men.

Viva Hukbalahap! Let us shout.

They shattered the dignity of our oppressed land,
They blighted our people with misfortune,
They killed those who opposed them,
Yet they say they are not our enemy
Because we belong to one race.)

Among the huk, no one used his or her real name. All the members were known by aliases. They gave me the name Bayang, the nickname for Maria, because my name is Maria Rosa.

The Huk explained that the Japanese Imperial Army invaded our country because we were an American colony. The US forces had their second largest military base in Pampanga, only six kilometers from our barrio. The Japanese wanted to free us from American colonialism, that was why they invaded countries like ours. But the Japanese failed to do good things in the occupied countries. They were oppressive and abusive.

The Hukbalahap did not rely on the United States during the war. The United States was very far away. The Filipinos did their best to fight the enemy. And where were the Americans?

After the fall of Bataan on April 9, 1942, General MacArthur, who led the American defense of the Philippines, President Manuel L. Quezon and other Filipino government officials fled to Australia from Corregidor on board a submarine. Before he left the Philippines, General MacArthur made his famous promise, "I shall return." Then he and the Filipino leaders went to the United States.

In the meantime, Filipinos were doing the fighting by themselves. The civilians lived in terror because of the Makapili who roamed with Japanese soldiers. If a Makapili said a person was a guerrilla, even if this person was innocent, he would be shot. That was why people were afraid to leave their homes, even to plant crops.

When we heard that Bataan had fallen, we all cried. Afterwards came the Death March, when the Japanese forced the captured Filipino and American soldiers to walk from Mariveles, Bataan, to the train station in San Fernando, Pampanga. From there, they boarded trains bound for Camp O'Donnell in Capas, Tarlac.

Some of my relatives were going to San Fernando to look for either a son or a brother who was in the Death March. I wanted to go with them and asked my mother's permission. We got up at dawn and took a cart pulled by a carabao until we reached the train station, about twenty kilometers away. We got there at about eight a.m.

At about noon, we saw the soldiers marching. Everyone cried in shock because the soldiers were very thin and pale, and looked too weak to march. Some of them could not even walk and could

The Bataan Death March.

stand up only with the support of their companions. If a soldier collapsed on the road, the Japanese just shot him to death.

There were hundreds of soldiers who passed, but we did not find the relatives we were looking for, so we headed home. All along the way, all I could think of was the Death March.

When we were on our way to our barrio, we saw a ten-year-old boy who was a member of our organization. He told us that many Japanese soldiers had raided our barrio and grabbed chickens, eggs, fruits and whatever else they could find.

It had been only three months since the Japanese landed. That early, we could foresee the misfortunes that were to befall us.

Shortly after the war broke out, the Japanese began to teach us their language and culture. Philippine magazines translated Japanese words into Pilipino. In school, children were taught their lessons in Japanese. And even though I was no longer studying, I learned a few Japanese words and letters from magazines like *Liwayway* and *Bulaklak*.

I still went to visit my father every month to collect the money he gave to support us. As before, I waited for him in the rice granary. All throughout the war, he did not renounce his obligation to us. I was grateful for his support, which we badly needed. He gave me Japanese money, which was the currency then in use.

One day my uncle Pedro, who worked in my father's big house, visited us to say that Don Pepe was going to evacuate to a distant town in Pampanga, about fifty kilometers from where we lived. The Japanese had asked him and his family to vacate their big house, which was being turned into the soldiers' headquarters. My father wanted to take my uncle with him.

My mother and I felt very sad. My mother did not want her brother to leave for a distant place. But my uncle insisted, saying he had to go so that our family would not lose contact with my father. As he was leaving, my mother said, "Pedro, do not forget to pray." Those days were filled with fear because there were many Japanese soldiers coming to our barrio with the Makapili spies. There were also many guerrillas in the barrio.

By now, English was rarely spoken. I heard people, especially students, speaking in Japanese. Vehicles were very rare. If we needed to go anywhere, we walked or took a carabao-drawn cart. The trains were always very full, people crammed even the top of the train cars. Only the Japanese Army had the fuel to run their trucks and other vehicles. Electricity was only for the Japanese Army.

Martial law had been declared, and a six p.m. to six a.m. curfew was strictly observed. People did as the Japanese ordered because anyone who violated their rules was punished. Some were tied to a post under the hot sun or held in a place crawling with ants.

We ate supper before twilight because we were not allowed to use even an oil light at night. The evenings were very dark because the Japanese forbade us to have lights in houses. Anyone walking at night with a candle or a torch was suspected of being a guerrilla. If we felt hungry, we ate boiled sweet potatoes in the dark.

My mother raised chickens, so we had eggs to eat and sometimes meat. We also had a little pig. But one day a member of the Makapili went to our house and took everything—the eggs, the chicken and the pig. He said that his Japanese companion had instructed him to get our animals. But we never saw his Japanese companion. My mother did not protest, she did not say a single word, she just gave him all we had. That was the way things were in our barrio.

The Makapili spy returned to our house in the forest a second time. I became worried because the guerrillas sometimes came to our house, too. If they encountered the Makapili there, my mother and I would be in trouble. An hour after the Makapili had left, a boy who served as a Huk courier told me that some guerrillas wanted to stop by our house. I told the boy that would be dangerous, as a Makapili had just been there and he might return.

The following morning, one of the women guerrillas came to our house to talk to my mother. "You must vacate this place," she told us. "The Makapili are spying on you because they suspect you have an underground connection." That same day, my mother and I, as well as her brother and a cousin who were living with us, left the hut in the forest. We took our belongings and stayed in the home of one of my mother's relatives in the same barrio. After one week, my mother and my uncle returned to our hut and found that it had been burned down, no one knew by whom.

We were in a very difficult situation, and we had to fend for ourselves. My uncle Pedro was with my father, and my three other uncles remained in Pasay. Emil, my youngest uncle, and I were the same age. The two of us helped some farmers harvest *kamote*, for which we got a share of the crop. Sometimes my mother sold *kamote* in the market so we could have money to buy oil for cooking and soap for washing our clothes.

When it was rice harvesting season, all of us—my mother, my uncle Emil and I—worked in the fields, gathering sheaves of rice so they could be threshed. At that time, threshing was done by men and women trampling on the rice plants to separate the grains from the stalk with their feet. We worked long hours under the heat of the sun so we could have a share of the harvest.

In the meantime, the war went on all around us. I continued to collect medicine and old clothes for the Huk, even though I feared being found out. Sometimes I heard from the guerrillas that some of our comrades had been tortured or beheaded by Japanese soldiers. Anyone suspected of having guerrilla connections was taken to the garrison, beaten up, tortured and killed. In a barrio not far from where we lived, five guerrillas were killed in an encounter with the Japanese Imperial Army.

We were careful not to be discovered by the Japanese. Our Huk meetings were held in different places in different barrios. Our commanders explained the situation to us. We should not rely on the promises of MacArthur, he said. "We are Filipinos and this is our land, we must fight for our freedom. We should not depend on the United States. We should not rely on anyone to save us. But we must always pray to God and have faith that one day we will have freedom."

The commander taught me what to do in case I encountered soldiers or spies. I was told to chew betel nut every time I went somewhere to collect medicine. Most of the old people in our barrio did this—they mixed the nut with some lime and *ikmo* leaves and then chewed the mixture, producing a red extract that colored their lips.

One day I was instructed to go to the town of Angeles to collect medicine from a guerrilla sympathizer. I carried a letter from my commander to prove to that person that I was with the Huk. The person I was to see had been informed of the day and time of my arrival.

Along the way, I saw two Japanese soldiers and a Makapili. I had kept the commander's letter hidden in the braid of my hair. I hurriedly took it out and chewed it with the betel nut mix. When I encountered the soldiers, the Makapili asked me where I was going. He looked suspiciously at the basket that I was carrying on top of my head. "I will sell these sweet potatoes in the market," I said.

They inspected the *kamote* one by one. Then they returned the basket to me and asked, "Have you seen any guerrillas in this place?"

"No," I answered.

Then they went on their way and I on mine. I got a little worried because I had no more letter to show to the person I was to meet. Instead I got a dried twig from a tree and proceeded.

When I reached the person, I told him that I had eaten the letter. Then I broke the twig into seven pieces. This was a prearranged code. The moment I did that, the man believed I was the guerrilla courier. The man gave me tablets for malaria and diarrhea and a bottle of disinfectant for wounds. I wrapped the medicine in my shawl, which was made of a discarded flour sack, and knotted it around my belly so that I would look pregnant. I was lucky that day because I got back home without any danger. That night, five guerrillas came to fetch the medicine.

My mother knew about my activities and was sympathetic to the guerrillas. Many others in our barrio were guerrilla contacts. One day I saw three women sitting next to each other on the steps fronting their house. They looked like they were looking for lice on each other's hair. But all of them faced east. It was a sign: there were guerrillas to the east.

Encountering Japanese soldiers and a Filipino informant as I was on a courier mission collecting medicine for the guerrillas.

It was my task to make sure that the guerrillas had food to eat. I went around the different houses, asking them to spare some food. Later I collected what the barrio people had prepared—food wrapped in banana leaves, enough to fill a jute sack. Before long, someone came to collect the food and take it to the guerrilla base.

For one year, I worked secretly for the Hukbalahap. It was work that gave me some fulfillment. But sometimes I felt very sad. I cried secretly, remembering what had been done to me. Whenever I sang the Hukbalahap song with my comrades, I felt deep hurt. There is a line in that song that refers to the abduction of women. It says:

> *Dapat lang itabi,*
> *ding pasistang Hapon a berdugo ping lahi,*
> *Kinamkam king pibandian,*
> *lepastangan da ing puri deting babai.*
> (They should be vanquished, the fascist Japanese,

the scourge of our race.
They seized our possessions and raped our women . . .)

When I sang that line, I whispered to myself, "I am one of those women." But nobody in the organization knew my secret.

4

COMFORT WOMAN

One morning in April 1943, I was asked by my Huk comrades to collect some sacks of dried corn from the nearby town of Magalang. I went with two others in a cart pulled by a carabao. One comrade sat with me in the cart, the other rode on the carabao's back. It was the height of the dry season. The day was very hot.

We loaded the sacks of corn into the cart and made our way back to our barrio. As we approached the Japanese checkpoint near the town hospital of Angeles, the man beside me whispered, "Be careful, there are some guns and ammunition hidden in the sacks of corn." I froze. I did not know till then that what we were sitting on were guns. I became very nervous, fearing that if the Japanese soldiers discovered the weapons, we would all get killed.

I got off the cart and showed the sentry our passes. At that time, everyone in the barrio needed to have a pass to show that he or she lived there. The sentry looked at the sacks of corn, touching here and pressing there without saying anything.

Finally, he allowed us to pass, but after we had gone thirty meters from the checkpoint he whistled and signaled us to return. We looked at each other and turned pale. If he emptied the sack, he would surely find the guns and kill us instantly. The soldier raised his hands and signaled that I was the only one to come back, and my companions were allowed to go. I walked to the checkpoint, thinking the guns were safe but I would be in danger. I thought that maybe they would rape me.

The guard led me at gunpoint to the second floor of the building that used to be the town hospital. It had been turned into the Japanese headquarters and garrison. I saw six other women there. I was given a small room with a bamboo bed. The room had no door, only a curtain. Japanese soldiers kept watch in the hall outside. That night, nothing happened to me.

The following day was hell. Without warning, a Japanese soldier entered my room and pointed his bayonet at my chest. I thought he was going kill me, but he used his bayonet to slash my dress and tear it open. I was too frightened to scream. And then he raped me. When he was done, other soldiers came into my room, and they took turns raping me.

Twelve soldiers raped me in quick succession, after which I was given half an hour to rest. Then twelve more soldiers followed. They all lined up outside the room waiting for their turn. I bled so much and was in such pain, I could not even stand up. The next morning, I was too weak to get up. A woman brought me a cup of tea and breakfast of rice and dried fish. I wanted to ask her some questions, but the guard in the hall outside stopped us from saying anything to each other.

Smuggling guns and ammunition in sacks of corn past the Japanese checkpoint. I wore a salakot to protect me from the sun's heat.

I could not eat. I felt much pain, and my vagina was swollen. I cried and cried, calling my mother. I could not resist the soldiers because they might kill me. So what else could I do? Every day, from two in the afternoon to ten in the evening, the soldiers lined up outside my room and the rooms of the six other women there. I did not even have time to wash after each assault. At the end of the day, I just closed my eyes and cried. My torn dress would be brittle from the crust that had formed from the soldiers' dried semen. I washed myself with hot water and a piece of cloth so I would be clean. I pressed the cloth to my vagina like a compress to relieve the pain and the swelling.

Every Wednesday, a Japanese doctor came to give us a check-up. Sometimes a Filipino doctor came. The other women could rest for four or five days a month while they had their period. But I had no rest because I was not yet menstruating.

The garrison did not have much food. We ate thrice a day, our meals consisting of a cup of rice, some salty black beans and thin pieces of preserved radish. On rare occasions, we had a hard-boiled egg. Sometimes there was a small piece of fried chicken. Sometimes we also had a block of brown sugar. I would suck it like candy or mix it with the rice, and I was happy. I kept the sugar in my room.

A soldier always stood in the hall outside the seven rooms where we were kept. The guard gave us tea every time we wanted some to drink. Once, he told me to wash my face with tea so that my skin would look smooth. He was kind to all the women there.

We began the day with breakfast, after which we swept and cleaned our rooms. Sometimes, the guard helped. He fixed my bed and scrubbed the floor with a wet cloth and some disinfectant. After cleaning, we went to the bathroom downstairs to wash the only dress we had and to bathe. The bathroom did not even have a door, so the soldiers watched us. We were all naked, and they laughed at us, especially at me and the other young girl who did not have any pubic hair.

Twelve soldiers raped me in quick succession.

I felt that the six other women with me also despised the Japanese soldiers. But like me, there was nothing they could do. I never got to know them. We just looked at each other, but were not allowed to talk. Two of the women looked Chinese. They always cast their gaze downward and never met my eye.

The only time I saw them was when we were taken for our daily bath and when, twice a week, we were taken out to get some sun. After bathing, we went back to our rooms. I would hang up my dress to dry and comb my long hair. Sometimes I sat on the bamboo bed, remembering all that had been done to me. How could I escape or kill myself? The only thing that kept me from committing suicide was the thought of my mother.

At around eleven, the guard brought each of us our lunch. He returned an hour later to collect our plates. Then a little before two in the afternoon, he brought us a basin with hot water and some pieces of cloth.

The guard gives me a cube of brown sugar.

At two in the afternoon, the soldiers came. Some of them were brought by truck to the garrison. My work began, and I lay down as one by one the soldiers raped me. At six p.m., we rested for a while and ate dinner. Often I was hungry because our rations were so small. After thirty minutes, I lay down on the bed again to be raped for the next three or four hours. Every day, anywhere from ten to over twenty soldiers raped me. There were times when there were as many as thirty: they came to the garrison in truckloads. At other times, there were only a few soldiers, and we finished early.

Most of the soldiers looked so young, maybe they were only eighteen years old. Their hair was cut short, only half an inch long. Most of them were clean and good looking, but many of them were rough.

I lay on the bed with my knees up and my feet on the mat, as if I were giving birth. Once there was a soldier who was in such a hurry to come that he ejaculated even before he had entered me.

He was very angry, and he grabbed my hand and forced me to fondle his genitals. But it was no use, because he could not become erect again. Another soldier was waiting for his turn outside the room and started banging on the wall. The man had no choice but to leave, but before going out, he hit my breast and pulled my hair.

It was an experience I often had. Whenever the soldiers did not feel satisfied, they vented their anger on me. Sometimes a soldier took my hand and put it around his genitals so I could guide him inside me. I soon learned that was the quickest way to satisfy the men and get the ordeal over with. But there was a soldier who did not like this. When I put my hand on his groin, he slapped me. He was very rough, poking his penis all over my genitals, even my backside, because he could not find my vagina. He kept pressing against my clitoris which got so swollen that I was in pain for three days. Even the hot water compress I made could not relieve the pain.

Some soldiers punched my legs and belly after they had ejaculated prematurely, staining their pants with their semen. One sol-

The soldiers watch us bathe and laugh at us.

dier raped me, and when he was finished, ordered me to fondle his genitals. He wanted to rape me a second time, but could not get an erection. So he bumped my head and legs against the wall. It was so painful. As he was hitting me, the soldiers outside started knocking impatiently on the wall. Through the thin curtain, I could see their impatient figures huddled in the hall.

Every day there were incidents of violence and humiliation. These happened not only to me, but also to the other women there. Sometimes I heard crying and the sound of someone being beaten up as there was only a partition made of woven bamboo that divided my room from those of the others.

When the soldiers raped me, I felt like a pig. Sometimes they tied up my right leg with a waist band or belt and hung it on a nail

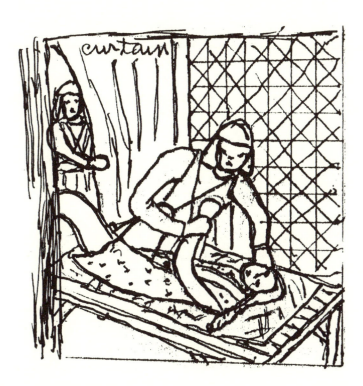

Every day this was the scene in my room.

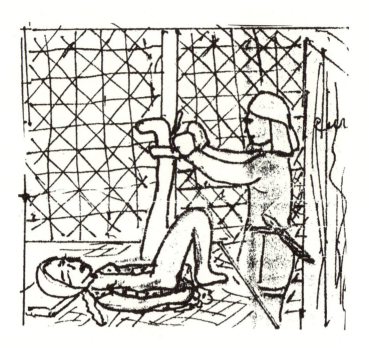

Sometimes the soldiers tied up my leg with a belt which they hung on a nail on the wall.

on the wall as they violated me. I was angry all the time. But there was nothing I could do. How many more days, I thought. How many more months? Someday we will be free, I thought. But how?

I thought of my guerrilla activities and my comrades. I regretted passing the sentry where the Japanese soldiers saw me. Did my comrades know that I was still alive and undergoing such horrible suffering? Maybe not. Was there anything they could do, I wondered. Sometimes I lost all hope.

I was in the hospital building for three months. Afterwards, in August of 1943, we were transferred to a big rice mill four blocks from the hospital. The mill was on Henson Road, named after my father's family, who owned the land where it stood. We found seven small rooms ready for each of us. The daily routine of rape continued. All throughout my ordeal, I kept thinking of my mother. Did she know I was still alive? How could I get in touch with her?

In December 1943, a new set of officers took over the mill. One day I saw the new captain. His face was familiar. I knew I had seen him before. Once the officer called me and asked, "Are you the girl whom I met in Fort McKinley?"

I bowed my head and answered, "Yes." It was the man who had raped me two years before. He told me his name was Captain Tanaka.

I cried every night, calling my mother silently.

The officers also demanded our services. Once they took all seven of us to a big house where they lived. That house belonged to my father, and it was where my mother worked while she was in her teens. We stayed there for an hour, and there we were raped. Tanaka was there, and so was his commanding officer, a colonel who raped me twice. We returned to the rice mill on board a truck guarded by soldiers. Sometimes we were transported to another big, old house where the other officers lived, and there we would again be raped.

Tanaka seemed to be fond of me, but I did not like him. He took pity on me. It seemed that if he could only stop the soldiers from raping me, he would. Sometimes, if the colonel was not there, he asked me to make some tea for him. He told me that he was from Osaka. He was about thirty-two years old, with eyes so small that they disappeared when he smiled.

From the time he recognized me as the girl he had raped in Fort McKinley, Tanaka became very kind to me. He could speak a little English, and he talked to me often. He asked me my name. "My name is Rosa," I answered. "Rosa means a flower, a rose."

From that time on, he called me Bara which means rose in Japanese, he said. He also asked me how old I was. I told him fifteen by making a sign with my fingers.

Many days passed. I looked at the calendar which hung in a hall outside my room. I realized Christmas was coming in a week. I remembered my mother again. I cried quietly. I missed my mother, and my father, too. Neither of them knew what had happened to me. Sometimes I stayed up all night, thinking about my parents. When morning came, it was back to the old routine.

Even the Japanese doctor who checked me every week did not spare me. Once, after the check-up, he asked me to stay behind. And then he raped me. I cried and cried because it hurt so much. His penis was very big.

By now I had served thousands of soldiers. Sometimes I looked at myself in the small mirror in my room and saw that what I had been through was not etched in my face. I looked young and pretty. God, I thought, how can I escape from this hell? Please God, help me and the other girls free ourselves from here.

We were still taken regularly to the big houses where the officers stayed. The old colonel would always choose me from among the other girls and rape me twice. He did not talk to me. He just gave me a cup of tea with sugar and a big banana and signaled me to eat it.

One morning, after I had cleaned my room, bathed and washed my only dress and towel, Tanaka called me to his room. I was combing my hair. "Bara, come here," he said. I sat in front of his table.

He was writing a letter with a fountain pen which he dipped in ink. Then he held my chin. He dipped his pen in the ink and pierced me with the tip of the pen. It was painful, as if I had been pricked by a needle. To this day, that ink mark is on my chin.

I do not know why he did that. He also ran his fingers through my hair. Then, when he saw a small cockroach on the table, he swatted it and burned it with a lighted cigarette. "*Moyasu*," he said, meaning burn. Just then, we heard the sound of a vehicle coming to a halt. Tanaka stood up and told me to go back to my room. He gave me two pieces of mint candy before I left.

The colonel had arrived. He headed straight for Tanaka's room. It was close to eleven a.m., and soon the guard came with my ration. It looked good—I had a piece of fried chicken, some vegetables and an egg. I kept the egg to eat before I went to sleep.

But as I was finishing my lunch, the colonel came into my room and raped me. I was scared because he looked very cruel. Afterward, he also gave me a piece of mint.

There was nothing we could do about our situation. After some time, I became very ill. I was getting chills, my fingernails were turning black, and I was always feeling thirsty. I could feel that I was going to have a malaria attack. But no matter how weak I was, the soldiers continued to rape me, and I was afraid they would hit me again even if I was very sick.

Then I developed a high fever. Tanaka found out I was ill, maybe because he could hear me crying and tossing in bed. He took me to his room and gave me a tablet for high fever. The colonel also found out. He visited me in Tanaka's room and told him that I was not to give service to the soldiers that day.

I was given my dinner in Tanaka's room, but I had no appetite. Tears just fell from my eyes. I was quiet. Tanaka looked at me sadly. I returned to my room at about ten p.m. I could not sleep the whole night, I just cried silently. I remembered my mother again and the thousands of soldiers who had raped me. I recalled their cruelty, their habit of hitting me when they were not satisfied with having raped me. I felt very weak.

I felt then that only Captain Tanaka understood my feelings. He was the only one who did not hurt me or treat me cruelly. But inside in my heart I was still very angry with him.

Sometimes, when the colonel was not in the garrison, Tanaka went to my room to talk to me, asking me if I felt better after my malaria attack. He would hold my face and look straight into my eyes. But I did not look at him. Sometimes I pitied him.

Since he understood a little English, I pleaded with him to allow me to escape. He said he could not let me go because it was against his vow. He could not do anything against the Emperor. Then he embraced me and kissed my cheeks and neck tenderly. Maybe he pitied me but could do nothing.

Even now I sometimes recall the things that Tanaka did for me. I remember the word "*Bara.*" I have told my granddaughter about this, and she and her mother sometimes call me Lola Bara instead of Lola Rosa.

One day, at about nine in the morning, I was combing my hair and had my back to the door. Suddenly I felt someone holding my hips. I was frightened. It was Tanaka. He started kissing my hair. Then he made me lie down on the bed and raped me.

I was very angry, and I was still feeling weak from malaria. Although he was not as rough as the others, he still took advantage of me. When he finished, he said, "*Arigato,*" and left. I understood what he meant. "Thank you," he said for the first time.

Once when a soldier was raping me, I suddenly got a malaria attack. I started shaking, and the soldier kicked me. I fell down

"Please, Tanaka, let me go."

from my bed to the floor. Maybe he thought that I was just pretending to be ill. But I kept on shivering, and I could feel that even my intestines were quivering.

The other soldiers waiting outside the room saw what happened. Captain Tanaka also noticed that something was wrong. He went to my room, picked me up from the floor and put me back on the bed. He wrapped a blanket around me and drew open the curtain that hung on my door. The soldiers waiting outside walked away.

The next day, the doctor came and confirmed that I had malaria. I was allowed to rest for a week. I was given two yellow tablets to take twice a day. But I still got malaria attacks every other day. After a week of taking the medicine, I began bleeding profusely. The Japanese doctor was not there, so Captain Tanaka found a

My malaria attack. The soldier raping me thought I was fooling him and kicked me.

Filipino doctor. He told me that I had a miscarriage. When I learned that I had lost a child, I began wondering how that was possible, as I had not yet begun to menstruate. And who was the father?

A week after my miscarriage, I was put back to work again. Even if I still had occasional malaria attacks, the soldiers continued to rape me. Sometimes, when the colonel was away, Captain Tanaka kept me in his room and hung up the curtain in my room so I could rest. When they saw the curtain up, the soldiers thought I was away. Captain Tanaka told them that I was in the hospital because I was sick. The captain did not rape or touch me while I was in his office.

One late morning, Tanaka asked me to bring two cups of tea to his room. On my way there, I overheard him and the colonel talking. By now, I could understand some Japanese although I could not speak it. I heard the two men say that they were planning to conduct a zoning operation in Pampang, our barrio, because many of the residents there were guerrillas. Our soldiers had captured guerrillas from there, and they were in the garrison downstairs, said the colonel.

At that point, I walked calmly into the room and put the two cups of tea on the table. As I was walking out, I heard the colonel say, "We will set fire to Pampang." I understood because he used the word *moyasu* which, I had learned from Tanaka, meant burn. I was crying in my heart. The first thought that came to my mind was my mother who lived there. Pampang was just six kilometers from the rice mill where I was held captive. How could I get word to my mother that the entire barrio would be burned?

I knew how cruel the Japanese Imperial Army could be. When they burned down a village, they had their machine guns ready to shoot at anybody fleeing the fire, especially if they found guerrillas there. Even rats and cats were killed.

Two o'clock came, and my daily ordeal with the soldiers began. That night I could not sleep. In the morning, as the sun rose, the soldiers went for their daily exercise. *"Miyo tokai kono sorakete!"* they shouted. When the routine was over, they shouted *"Banzai!"* three times.

I was in luck that day because the guards took us downstairs so we could have some sunshine. The seven of us went down to the open field where the soldiers had their exercises. The field fronted the street, but the Japanese had fenced it off with barbed wire so no one could escape. The three guards with us were laughing and joking. I walked close to the street and saw an old man pass by. His face looked familiar to me, and I knew that he lived in our barrio.

"Tonight your barrio will be burned," I whispered to him while the guards were not looking. "Get out of there." Then I quickly turned away, pretending there was nothing the matter. Later we were sent back to our rooms for our daily routine—cleaning, bathing, washing.

At lunch I could hardly swallow my food. I was very tense. The soldiers lined up outside my room as usual. I finished at nine in the evening. While I was in my room resting, I noticed that the

Tied up, along with guerrilla captives, for torture.

colonel and the captain were leaving the building with some soldiers. I heard their vehicles driving away. Some of the soldiers
remained to guard us.

After more than an hour, I heard the colonel and Tanaka rush-
ing up the stairs. The colonel grabbed me from my bed and
slapped me hard. My eyes swelled and there was blood on my
face. The colonel was very angry because when they reached Pampang, there was not a single soul there. He suspected that it was I
who had frustrated their plans, as I was the only one who had
heard them talking.

I was dragged downstairs to the garrison where the colonel
beat me up, tied my hands with a rope and hung them on the wall.

Beaten by the colonel.

I forced my eyes open to see what was around me. I saw some guerrilla captives. They also had many bruises and, like me, their hands were tied up.

When daylight came, I was very thirsty, and my entire body was in pain from the torture that I had undergone. At noon, the colonel went down to the garrison to inspect the prisoners. He poured water on our faces. I welcomed every drop of water that reached my parched lips. My throat was dry, and I eagerly drank up the water.

Then suddenly I felt very cold. I knew that I was going to have another malaria attack. I was shivering, but my hands were still tied up. My whole body was shaking, and I wanted to lie down. I cried, "I want to die now." Then the high fever came, and I thought I could not remain standing for long. My head was aching and felt so heavy, I could barely hold it up.

Someone held up my chin. I forced my swollen eyes to open. I saw Captain Tanaka giving me a cup of tea. He held the cup to my lips, but suddenly the colonel came down shouting. He bumped my head against the corrugated iron wall of the rice mill. I passed out.

I was still unconscious when the guerrillas attacked the garrison. My mother would tell me later that the Huks assaulted the rice mill that night to free their imprisoned comrades. They found me there still chained, and they freed me as well. One guerrilla carried me with him as the Japanese soldiers pursued him. Unable to carry me any farther, the Huk dropped me in a shallow ditch on the roadside. Fortunately, it was a moonlit night, and Anna, my mother's cousin, lived nearby. She was up late preparing the *kamote* she was going to sell in the market the following day. The moon lit up the road fronting her house, and she saw me sprawled on the roadside. She informed my mother, who promptly came to get me.

The first thing I remembered when I regained consciousness was the colonel shouting and bumping my head because Captain Tanaka was giving me something to drink. I had difficulty talking, but the first thing I asked my mother was, "What happened to the six women, my companions in the garrison? Were they killed? Did they escape?" But my mother did not know.

It was January 1944. I had been held captive as a sex slave for nine months.

My mother, Julia, at my baptism.

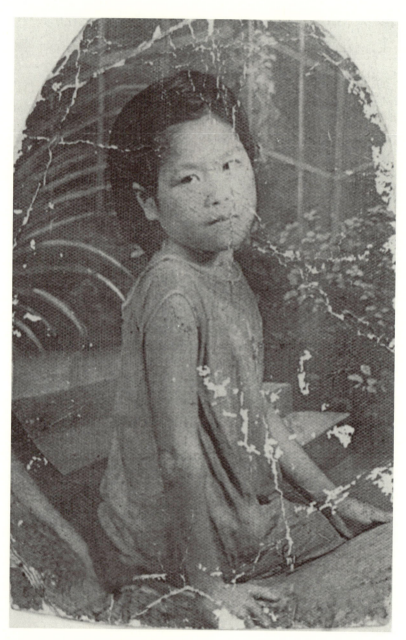

A photograph of me at age seven.

My husband, Domingo, and I with our children, Rosario and Rosalinda, in 1950.

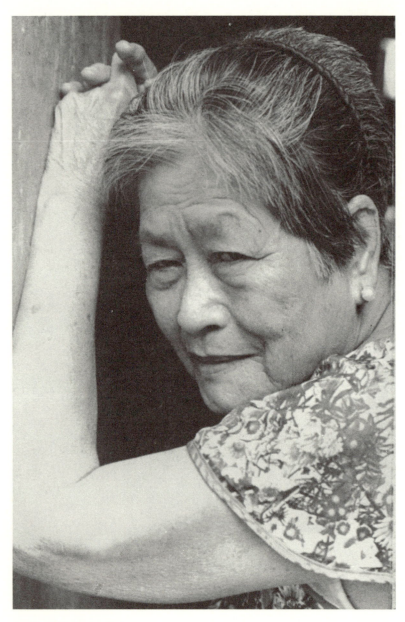

At home in March 1996.

5

PAIN AND RECOVERY

I regained consciousness only two months after I was rescued from the garrison. I found myself in my mother's house. I wept when I saw my mother's face. I wanted to speak, but no words came from my mouth. I did not say a word for a long time.

My mother nursed me back to health, spoon-feeding me as if I were a baby. I could neither stand nor walk. I crawled like an infant. I could not focus my eyes well, and everything I saw was blurred.

I refused to show myself to anybody except my mother. I was always hiding in a corner of the room. Slowly, I began to remember everything that had happened to me. I could see clearly the faces of Captain Tanaka, the colonel, and the six women I was with. I cried and cried, and my mother tried to comfort me.

Every time I spoke, I began to drool, my saliva dripping from the corner of my mouth like a dog. My mother pitied me very much. I wept not only for my pain, but for hers. I tried to write so I could explain what had happened to me, but the pencil would drop from my fingers, and the words I wrote came out badly. For years, I had difficulty writing. I practiced hard to perfect my writing, but even now my pen sometimes slips, and the letters become garbled.

I stumbled when I walked, and for years afterward I would lose my balance. Sometimes I still got malaria attacks. My mother boiled some herbal medicine to help me heal.

Despite my speech difficulties, I managed to tell my mother all that had happened to me. My mother cried bitterly. She and I were very close, and I shared with her all my secrets.

One day, one of my mother's cousins came to visit. I kissed her hand to show my respect, but my saliva dripped on her hand. She looked at me with pity. "My dear niece, what kind of sickness do you have?" My mother explained that I was stricken with malaria and high fever, and that I was tortured by the soldiers. She never told them that I had been repeatedly raped.

"Maybe her brain was damaged," my aunt cried as she embraced and kissed me. I cried, too, and so did my mother. Then I went to my room, sobbing. I thought once more of the six women I was with and of the Japanese soldiers. Once again I regretted having passed the Japanese sentry the day I went out on a mission. But I had to accept my fate.

My mother kept me hidden at home for fear that if the Japanese Army found me, both of us would be killed. For years, I was constantly haunted by nightmares. I envied other girls my age who were always smiling and looked very happy, innocently enjoying the songs and the dances and the company of their friends, while I was hiding at home.

For a year, my mouth was hanging open, and my saliva was dripping down the side of my face. I had difficulty speaking. Even my hair started falling. The mere sight of men made me run and hide. I thought all men were oppressive like Japanese soldiers. I also felt unworthy because to my mind, I had become soiled and dirty from repeated rape.

On September 1, 1944, my mother took me back to Pasay so I could see our family doctor. We traveled on the roof of the train because there were so many passengers. The doctor examined me as my mother narrated my ordeal. He said that I fell unconscious because of the blow to my head and the malaria fever. He told me I was lucky to have survived. "Just pray that Rosa will not lose her memory and her sanity," he told my mother. "Otherwise, she would become forgetful or worse, she might go mad."

When I heard these words from that doctor's mouth, I vowed to do everything in my power so that I would not lose my sanity.

I was the center of jokes then because of my speech difficulty. My neighbors thought that I had gone mad. Even my own mother, who was the only one who knew my secrets, was beginning to think that I was crazy because I kept muttering to myself, "Why did I not escape? Because they might kill me."

I became afraid of people who I thought were against me and talking behind my back. I became ashamed of myself. I lost my self-confidence and self-respect. I felt like hiding from people all the time. I wanted to bury my head in the ground. I had to fight a constant struggle with myself to remain alive and to keep my sanity.

Then on September 21, 1944, there was an airfight. With my own eyes, I saw the planes firing at each other. By then we had run out of food. So in October we returned to Angeles on foot. There were many other people walking. It took us a week to get there.

The US and Allied forces landed in Leyte on October 22, 1944. We were thrilled with the news that General MacArthur had fulfilled his promise to return. He came back, landing in Leyte with Allied soldiers, warships and hundreds of planes. The battles between Japanese and Allied soldiers were fierce and lasted for weeks. We were in Angeles by then. At night, we were woken by the sound of bombing. We ran to our air raid shelter to avoid the Allied bombardment.

On January 9, 1945, General MacArthur made another landing, this time in Lingayen Gulf. My mother told me that somebody had given her the news. Air raids were now taking place almost every day and night. Sometimes my mother, my uncle Emil and I spent the entire day in the air raid shelter. In our area, the Japanese Imperial Army became even more strict and cruel. We heard that massacres were taking place everywhere.

Just before Christmas that year, my uncle Pedro visited us. He came with my father's permission. My mother was very happy to see him. He handed her an envelope full of Japanese money from Don Pepe. He said the landlord had asked my mother and me to always pray and to be careful.

Pedro was very sad to learn that I had been ill. He recounted that he had walked for three days because there were no more trains or cars to board. He decided not to return to where my father was staying.

The battles between the Japanese Imperial Army and the Allied forces were now taking place more and more often. One early morning, a Japanese soldier knocked on our door with his rifle. "*Tetsudai*," he called. We understood that the word meant helper. The soldier took my two uncles and me, whom he mistook for a boy because most of my hair had fallen off, and I was dressed like a man. My mother could not do anything to stop him.

The soldiers put us in a truck with many other boys and girls. The truck proceeded to Fort Stotsenberg, passing through our barrio. We arrived in the camp after an hour. We were ordered to work there, loading boxes of food or ammunition inside a big tunnel.

They gave us lunch—a cup of rice and a piece of dried fish. But I could not swallow the food because I was very nervous and afraid, remembering my ordeal. In the afternoon, they loaded us into the truck again and took us home. We reached home at twilight. At that time, there were no lights. There was a blackout, and only the Japanese had electricity.

That night, we slept in our air raid shelter. We hid there, thinking we could evade the Japanese soldiers. But the next morning, the same soldier was there again, knocking on our air raid shelter. We could not resist, so we boarded the truck again.

But as we drove on, we encountered two US fighter planes in the middle of the road. The Japanese soldiers ordered us to remove our hats. The pilot of the American plane saw that we were Filipinos, so he let the truck pass. We expected him to shoot. The soldier who was with us already had his eyes closed, and his hands were covering his ears. The truck moved very slowly. My uncle pinched my hand, and he crawled quietly out of the truck. I crawled out, too, as did my other uncle. The truck drove away, and the soldiers did not see us escaping.

We walked through a ricefield and past tall grasses. We moved quietly until we reached our house. It was almost dark. Later, we decided to move to another house for safety.

The next morning, a man whose two sons had been in the truck with us asked my uncle where our companions were. Those people were never found. Later, one of those who had been there recounted that the Japanese soldiers killed everyone who had helped them load food and ammunition into the tunnel.

We woke up to the sound of gunfire in the early morning of January 26, 1945. Then at about seven o'clock, as my mother, my two uncles and I were eating a breakfast of boiled *kamote* and water, three Japanese Army soldiers barged into our house. One of the soldiers pointed his pistol at my uncles and held them captive in the room downstairs. The other one dragged my mother and me to the yard at the back of the house and tied our hands behind our backs.

We saw three more soldiers in the yard and witnessed them gunning down nine men at random. It was close to the end of the war, and the Japanese were on a retreat. They were getting desperate, so they were shooting people everywhere. Later we saw the men's corpses sprawled in the ricefield behind our house.

The soldiers were approaching us, and my mother and I knew we were the next to be shot. Suddenly two men with loads on their backs ran past us. The soldiers saw them and chased them, leaving my mother and me alone. We were praying the "Our Father" very loudly, our eyes looking up at the sky. Then I told my mother, "We must run away now." But my mother was reluctant to leave. "If the Japanese soldiers return, they will kill us," I insisted. "Maybe God is giving us a chance to escape from here."

So we ran and hid in the air raid shelter we had dug under our house. There, we untied each other's hands. After some time, my two uncles returned, and when we saw them, my mother and I cried. Thank God we were all safe.

Japanese soldiers invade our house and hold us at gunpoint. They did not notice I was a girl because I wore boy's clothing and my hair had grown only half an inch since I became bald.

My uncles related that the soldiers had taken them for questioning to their headquarters in the rice mill. There, a Japanese officer, a colonel, told them that if they wished to evacuate, they should not head north because American troops were already in Dagupan, Pangasinan. Miraculously, they were released.

I was scared. The colonel who had raped me was still around, I thought, and so were the soldiers. I wondered about Tanaka. Was he still there as well? My mother saw me shaking and embraced me. "Do not worry too much," she whispered.

After a while, we thought it was safe enough to leave the air raid shelter. As we were going out, we saw Anna, my mother's cousin, who lived only three houses away. She was calling out to my mother. "Julia, please help me," she said crying. She told us about her husband William, the American soldier she had married long before the war broke out. "I need your help. I want to take

We prayed very loudly, looking up at the sky.

William with me to evacuate to the forest. He might be killed if the Japanese soldiers see him here."

William, a former soldier stationed in Fort Stotsenberg, had retired from the US Army and set up his own business. He and Anna did not have children although they adopted some of Anna's nephews and nieces. Soon after the war began, Anna hid William in the ceiling of their house. He had been there for three years. He was ill from the heat and the lack of exercise; he could barely walk or talk. No one except Anna knew where he was. At the start of the war, the Japanese had rounded up all the Americans and put them in prisons or concentration camps. William would have been tortured in one of those camps, too, if Anna had not hidden him.

As the months passed, things became increasingly difficult, and there was hardly anything to eat. Anna agreed to live with another man so she and William could survive. Her adopted children were married and could manage on their own. She smuggled food to her husband and kept him alive for three years.

Now, when it was no longer safe to remain in the village, she wanted our help to rescue him. My two uncles were not convinced. "We cannot be seen with William. The Japanese will kill us," they said. But we agreed to accompany Anna to her house.

There we saw William crawling on the floor. He had jumped down from the ceiling.

"We cannot take him with us," my uncle said. "We'll all get killed." William tried to hold my mother and looked up at her with tears flowing from his eyes. My mother cried, and so did Anna and I. My two uncles decided to leave. But my mother was firm. "I will not leave William, I will stay here with him even if I get killed."

My uncles stopped and listened. "Maybe God saved me and Rosa from the soldiers who were about to kill both of us, so we can save William's life," my mother said.

So my uncles made a hammock out of bed sheets and a thick bamboo pole. They put William on the hammock and covered him with pillows and kitchen utensils. We knew that we were all risking our lives. We left our village on foot, with my mother, Anna and me walking behind my two uncles carrying the hammock. We were nervous and in tears. We prayed the "Our Father" along the way.

At dusk, we passed a sentry. The Japanese soldiers halted us. One of them poked at the hammock with his bayonet. Luckily, he struck a pillow, and all the fluffy cotton inside it fell all around us. Irritated, the soldier let us go.

We walked away safe. Then my two uncles started running, carrying the hammock with them. We ran to catch up with them. It was getting dark. Along the way, the bamboo pole broke, and the five of us had to hold on to the four corners of the bed sheet, carrying poor William. We threw away the pillows and the other things to lighten our load.

When we finally reached the village where we were going to stay, we found many other evacuees there. When they saw William, they became angry. "You bring us a pest," they said. "If the Japanese find him, we might all be killed." All of them left us, even Anna's adopted children who had arrived there before we did.

That night we hid. William crawled into an air raid shelter and stayed there with Anna. My mother, my two uncles and I hid in another shelter. The whole night we could not sleep because of the noise. We heard shots being fired, airplanes flying to and fro, even the crackle of houses burning. We knew that the Allied forces were driving the Japanese away.

In the morning, we ate raw *kamote*. We ventured out of the shelter which was very hot and full of mosquitoes. The village was deserted. We crawled on the ground until we reached a field of tall grass near a small river. We witnessed an air battle, and all around Japanese soldiers were burning houses and shooting people.

The allied forces reached Angeles, Pampanga, on January 27, 1945. It was a Saturday. Everyone was happy. People greeted the soldiers with a smile and a salute of "Victory Joe." Anna was very happy, too. She kissed my mother, my two uncles and me with tears of joy in her eyes.

People were returning to the village now. Anna's adopted sons came, offering to take William out of the shelter. But he refused to even look at them. William crawled out of the shelter by himself and embraced my two uncles. He was in tears. He approached my mother and kissed her on the forehead. Some of the villagers who witnessed the scene were in tears themselves.

The American soldiers gave us boxes of C-rations. We were very hungry. When night fell, we moved around quietly, careful not to make any noise, lest we be the target of Japanese snipers. The Allied soldiers were sleeping all around us, and they expected that the Japanese would shoot at them. We decided to return to our own village the next day.

At about seven o'clock the following morning, my mother, my two uncles and I rode a carabao-drawn cart. We took Anna and William with us. We found a white sheet and made it fly like a banner on the cart. The road was full. People were going back to their homes.

We took Anna and William to their house and discovered that Japanese soldiers had been there. The meal Anna had cooked and left behind untouched before she left in a hurry had been eaten. We also saw two Japanese Army caps, a bayonet and a small Japanese flag. We knew instantly that if William had been left behind in that house, he would probably have been killed.

There were many American soldiers stationed in our village. Many of them visited William, who could not yet speak, so he communicated with his fingers. We found Allied soldiers in our own house, too. They gave us canned food and blankets. At night they slept outside, on hammocks covered with mosquito nets. I was still afraid of strangers then, so I hid in my room.

My two uncles worked as helpers with the Allied forces. They gave us some money and some food. My father was still in a distant town, and we had no idea what had happened to him. We received news that Manila had been liberated on February 5, 1945. Everyone was happy, it was like a feast.

I was happy, too, but I could not stop my tears. They were too late to save me from my ordeal, I thought. I was still crying in the middle of the night. My mother always came to comfort me. My hair, which had fallen off, had grown back, but it was still only half an inch long. I always covered my head with a big handkerchief so people would not see that I was bald. We had moved to Angeles from the barrio, so my mother and I could find work. We stayed in a house near the hospital where I had been held captive for three months.

At around this time, my father returned from the faraway town where he had spent most of the war years. My uncle Pedro went to see him in his big house. My father asked about my mother and me. Pedro told him that I wanted to see him. But he refused. "Not this time," he said, "because I have many things to do. Besides, my children know about Rosa now. They asked if I had a daughter with another woman. And I am troubled by their questions."

My father added, "Rosa is old enough now. She can live with her mother in whatever way they please." Pedro left, wondering about the meaning of those words.

I was sad when I heard what my father had said. I understood that he had to do what he felt was right. I knew he wanted to show his love and concern for me, but could not upset his family. My mother understood the situation, too. My father had, in effect, forsaken us. He felt that he had fulfilled his obligation to us. He gave me his name, and for years he supported not only me but also my mother's whole family. I did not expect to see him again.

We transferred to a house near the military camp in Angeles, where my mother and I could earn some money by doing the laundry for American and Filipino troops. We had no income anymore, and my mother also told me that we could no longer rely on my father's support.

We washed the clothes with our hands. It was also my task to iron the uniforms. I would iron them with tears in my eyes because they reminded me of the Japanese soldiers who had ruined my future.

I was always sad. Even my relatives and neighbors noticed how lonely I was. I was not interested in talking to them. And I was always guarded, wondering how they would react if they knew what had happened to me. Some soldiers would come to our house to fetch their laundry. But they never saw me because I was always hiding.

One day my mother talked to me. "Rosa, I want for you to get married," she said. I told her I had no feelings toward men. I said I hated the idea of love. But my mother urged me, saying marriage could help me forget my ordeal.

"Love will develop in due course," my mother said. I do not like to be in love, I whispered to myself. Then I began to think and think. I realized my mother's advice was for my own good. I thought it might be good to have children who would be with me when I grew old. I was an only child and could rely on no one else's help and comfort. My mother said I might go mad if I did not stop recalling the past and murmuring to myself. It was true. I often muttered questions to myself. Why did I not try to escape? I kept asking myself. And I would answer, because they might kill me.

6

MY MARRIED LIFE

As the days passed, I tried to get over my pain. My mother was a great comfort to me, and slowly I became hopeful about my life. My hair had grown back, and I became interested in the way I looked. I learned how to fix my clothes and my hair. I thought I looked young and pretty. My skin was fair and smooth, and my hair now fell to below my ears. It was the middle of 1945, and I was eighteen years old.

I had overcome my trauma somewhat, so I could now face the soldiers who came to fetch their laundry from our house. But I was still very angry with them because they reminded me of Japanese troops. There was a young soldier named Domingo who liked talking to me, but I could not talk much with him because I still had difficulty speaking. My words came out slurred and my saliva dribbled from my mouth.

Domingo visited our house every day. My mother became quite fond of him. He told her he was in love with me and wanted to marry me. He was very respectful, polite and thoughtful. He courted me by being nice and helpful. He fetched the soldiers' clothes from the camp and took them to our house to save my mother the trouble of going to the camp herself. He also delivered the clothes to the soldiers and collected the payment, which he handed over to my mother. My mother wanted him to be my husband. She did not mind that he was poor like us.

Domingo was born in Alaminos, Laguna, in 1925, and was two years older than I. His parents were peasants. They had no land of their own, so they worked in neighboring rice farms and coconut plantations. They had three children, and Doming was the middle child. He went to a public school in Alaminos and finished the seventh grade. He stopped schooling so he could help his father work in the farm.

Doming's father joined the guerrillas in 1942 and was killed in an encounter with Japanese soldiers in 1944. After his father's death, Doming himself joined his father's guerrilla unit. He was with the Allied forces fighting the Japanese Army in the mountains of Montalban, Marikina and San Mateo in Rizal. In May 1945, Allied troops set up camp in Angeles. Doming joined them there and worked as a waiter in the officers' mess hall of the Philippine Scouts, which was then under the US Army's 12th Division.

That was about the time he met my mother and me. He was a persistent suitor, but I had no feelings of love for him. I did not want to marry him. I only wanted to have a child so that when I grew old, someone would care for me. I confessed to him that I had been raped by Japanese soldiers, but I never told him that I also became a comfort woman.

Doming told me that the rape was a thing of the past and he still wanted to marry me. But I did not accept his proposal. I told him he was free to marry someone else. He was insistent, but I explained to my mother that I did not like to have a wedding. I still felt dirty because of what had happened to me. I thought of myself as the leavings of the Japanese.

I agreed to live with Doming in Angeles sometime in September 1945. A week afterward, we visited his mother in Laguna, who insisted that we be properly wed. I still refused, but could not stop her from arranging a simple civil ceremony in the town hall.

Doming did not force me to have sex with him; he would politely ask for it. But every time we had sex, the images of Japanese soldiers raping me would flash in my mind. I never enjoyed my sex life with my husband because of this. Often I would have nightmares of Japanese soldiers staring at me while I lay with my husband. They were sneering and shouting at me, forcing me to look at them.

I also had recurring dreams of Tanaka giving me a cup of tea. That last moment of consciousness before the Japanese colonel bumped my head against the wall of the rice mill kept replaying itself in my sleep.

Doming worked with the US Army 12th Division until it left for Okinawa, Japan, in 1946. My husband opted to stay behind and was later discharged from the Army. Later we moved to Pasay, where my husband and my uncles found work as laborers in the Department of Highways.

Everyday, I woke up early to cook rice and fish which Doming took with him to work. He was a *caminero*, a roving manual laborer who dug canals, repaired roads and swept the streets. If his job site was nearby, I would cook his meal later in the day and take it to him at lunch time. His work was not stable. He was a casual laborer, which meant that he was out of work every two weeks. After two weeks of not working, he was hired again. We could barely make ends meet, so my mother helped us by giving us some money for our daily needs. She was then working as a cook for a rich family.

In February 1947, when I was pregnant with my first child, one of my mother's relatives came to tell us that my father had died. My mother and I rushed to Angeles. When we got there, my father had been buried already; he had been dead a week. My mother and I went to the cemetery and put flowers on his tomb.

The next day, I went to the big house of my father. One of his sons saw me and led me upstairs. I saw an old woman sitting near the window. It was Doña Saring, my father's wife. I approached her and kissed her hand to show my respect. She did not know who I was and why I was there.

My father's son then led me to another room where I was confronted by the husband of my father's eldest daughter. "Who are you?" the man asked.

"I am the illegitimate daughter of Don Pepe," I answered humbly.

"Who is your mother?" he asked again.

"My mother is Julia, who was once the maid of the landlord and his wife," I said.

"Are you sure that Don Pepe was your father?"

"Yes, sir," I answered, "because we saw each other from the time I was a small girl. He sent me to school and gave me his name."

The man was angry now. "I do not believe that you are his daughter," he said, "because he cannot love another woman when he was already married. I know that you just want to ask for a share of his estate. Don't you know that Don Pepe died a poor man? That he had many loans?" He went on and on.

"I came here only to pay tribute to his kindness and concern," I said. "I cannot deny that he was my father." I spoke softly, but deep in my heart I was very angry with this man. I left quickly, and vowed never to return to that place again.

I did not bother to even think about my share of my father's estate. It was enough that he did his best to fulfill his obligations to me, my mother and her family while he was alive. I told my mother this, and she agreed. We stayed in Angeles for a week to mourn him.

Rosalinda, my eldest daughter, was born on August 13, 1947. She was followed by Rosario, who was born on September 2, 1949. I gave birth to both of them in a hospital about five kilometers from where we lived.

In 1949, Doming decided that we should move to his mother's hometown in Sta. Cruz, Laguna, where there was more work to be found. My mother remained in her small house in Pasay. She would visit us in Laguna once a month to see her two grandchildren and to bring some food or clothes for them.

My husband worked in the fields, harvesting coconut or making copra. In the rainy season, he planted rice. He built a small hut for us near his mother's house. He also planted some vegetables in our backyard, which we harvested and sold in the market. My husband was paid two pesos for a day's work in the field planting rice. But at that time, fifty kilos of rice was sold for only ten pesos, so we managed to survive.

I got along well with my mother-in-law who was widowed at a young age. After her husband died, she returned to her hometown and remarried. She and my own mother became good friends. My mother-in-law had a baby girl who was the same age as Rosalinda.

My husband and I got along well. He had a good sense of humor, and in many ways we were compatible. When he was not

My husband would sing love songs to our daughters.

working in the fields, he helped me take care of our daughters so I could do the washing and cooking. He liked to play with them. He would strum his guitar and sing them love songs. My son Jesus, who was born years later, inherited his father's musical talent. He is now a lead guitarist in a band, and his son is named Domingo, after his father.

My husband looked happy with his family. I attended to his needs and obeyed what he wanted me to do. I wanted to show him that I had healed. I was happy, too. For the first time since I was kept in the Japanese garrison, I was happy. I always remembered my mother's words, "Love develops in due course."

Doming knew that the past still haunted me. He would wake me up in the middle of the night whenever I had nightmares. Sometimes I called out in a loud voice, "Tanaka, don't leave me." My husband would shake me awake and ask me who Tanaka was. I would answer angrily, "I confessed to you all the things that had happened to me, but I don't know that Tanaka." I lied so there would be no more questions that I did not want to answer. My husband would just keep quiet and calm me down. But he looked sad. What should I have done? I asked myself. Was he jealous of the past? Sometimes I hated him because he knew how I had been defiled. But I continued to be nice to him, to serve him and please him. Maybe I even learned to love him.

One night in June 1950, when my younger daughter was about nine months old, we were awakened by loud knocking on the door. There were five armed men outside our house, and they were calling my husband.

Even before Doming and I had a chance to talk, the men took my husband away with them. I ran to my mother-in-law's house with my two daughters to tell them what had happened. The next morning, I went with my mother-in-law to report the incident to the police.

Many days passed, and there was no news about my husband. I had no idea where he was or who the armed men that night were. I did not know much about my husband's friends because whenever they visited us, I always pretended to be occupied in the kitchen. I was embarrassed to talk to them because my speech was still slurred.

I was worried not only for Doming, but also for our children. After five months of waiting, I decided to return to Pasay. I could not just stand and wait for my husband while my children went hungry, I told my mother-in-law.

In Pasay, I washed and ironed clothes in the house of a well-to-do family. I was paid two pesos a day. My mother took care of my daughters while I was away. I returned home at about five in the afternoon, happy to see my children with such a loving and caring grandmother.

I worked hard every day, striving to earn enough money so we could have enough to eat. Apart from doing laundry, I sewed dresses and mended clothes. None of our relatives or neighbors helped us. I stopped disturbing my mind with thoughts of my husband. As the days passed, I no longer hoped that he would return.

Then in March 1951, my daughter Rosario got very sick. She was vomiting continuously and suffering from diarrhea. I took her to the nearest hospital, and the doctor said there was poison in her blood. She needed to be confined, but we had no money. The hospital staff put her in the charity ward while my mother and I kept watch, sleeping on the chairs in the emergency room because we could not afford a room of our own.

The doctor said Rosario only had a fifty-percent chance of survival. My mother and I prayed that she would get well. After two weeks, he said Rosario was out of danger. He gave me a prescription for medicine, but I had no money. There was no one around to help me. Even my aunts and uncles, who had all lived off my father's support, did not offer any help.

I went to my mother-in-law in Laguna. I told her that Rosario was ill, and I showed her the doctor's prescription. She gave me money to buy the medicine, which I bought in the pharmacy in Sta. Cruz. As I was about to go to the bus station, two armed men approached me. One of them whispered in my ear, "Go with us without making any noise or else . . ." I was very scared. It was about four o'clock in the afternoon, and I was desperate to return to the hospital so I could take the medicine to Rosario.

One of the men took the medicine from me. They led me on a long hike through the mountains. We passed coconut farms and cogon fields. We walked for more than an hour until we reached a clearing where there were many huts made of bamboo and palm leaves. I saw my husband waiting for us. I tried to run toward him, but two armed men stopped me. Then I saw a beautiful woman standing near Doming. She asked the men, "Who is this woman? Why is she here? Do you know her name?"

Then the woman turned to my husband, "Who is this woman? Do you know her?"

"She is Rosa, my wife," he answered.

"Oh, I see," she said. "I hope you don't plan to let her live here. You know that our rules forbid men to have two wives." At that moment, I understood that my husband had another woman. I did not feel anger or jealousy. All that filled my mind at that moment were thoughts of my child and the medicine that she needed.

I started crying. I became angry with my husband for keeping me there. "You have forgotten your family," I sobbed. "Your daughter is sick, she is in the hospital. I came only to see your mother to ask for money for medicine. Why did you order your men to get me? Why have they brought me here?"

I kept asking questions. Doming only answered, "I do not know, Rosa, but I need you here."

"Let me go home," I cried, "or else I will report your whereabouts to the military."

The men around him were alarmed. "Then we cannot let you go," one of them said. "Is that not so, *Kumander*?" he asked my husband.

Doming told his men, "Treat her like a prisoner, not as the wife of your commander." Then he left. I wept. Again images of my captivity during the war flashed before my eyes. I pleaded, but my husband just walked away.

They took me to a hut. That night I could not sleep. I was tormented by the thought of Rosario being sick. Several men kept watch over me.

At that time I had not yet fully grasped the situation. Only later did I understand what had happened. One day a jacket that hung in one of the huts fell to the floor. I picked it up to hang it again, and I saw a small book fall from the pocket. It was a diary, and it was in my husband's handwriting.

"When the armed men took me from my house," it read, "they took me to the mountains. They wanted me to join them and threatened to kill me if I refused. I decided to be with them, in the hope that someday I would have a chance to escape and return to my family alive. They were outlaws fighting the government for their rights.

"Many days passed, and I learned more about this antigovernment movement and what I have learned has opened my eyes." I continued reading. "Until the day came when I became the commander of this movement. Maybe my family thinks that I am dead. I miss them very much." As I read those lines, I heard someone coming, so I put the book back.

I understood now that if my husband had not been abducted by the armed men, he would have been happy to live with us. I had no idea what he and his men were fighting for, nor was I concerned. All I could think of was Rosario, that if she did not get the medicine she needed, she might fall ill again and die. I was not distressed that Doming had found another woman. I understood his situation. He was probably lonely in the mountains. In one corner of my heart, I still loved him.

For the first three weeks that I was held captive, I did not see Doming. Then one day, there was a knock on my door. It was Doming. He talked with me cordially. He tried to explain his situation, that he was a commander of the HMB, the Hukbong Mapagpalaya ng Bayan, an armed group determined to fight the government and redistribute land to the peasants. Many of the HMB had been Huk guerrillas who fought against the Japanese.

I tried to escape but was re-captured.

As we were talking, a man came. He had with him the medicine I was carrying when I was abducted. Doming gave me the
medicine, and I sobbed. I held the small brown bag close to my
chest. "This medicine did not reach my sick child," I cried. "Is
Rosario still alive?" I wept so hard. My husband tried to comfort
me and hug me, but I turned away and cursed him. "I despise
you," I shouted. "Don't go near me. I hate you, get out of my
sight." I prayed to God that Rosario was safe and healthy.

The days passed. I spent them alone in a hut which was guarded night and day. But one day the guard was not there, so I attempted to escape. As I was walking in the forest, one of the men saw me. He ran after me, but I ran even faster. Then I saw that there were now five men trying to get me. One of them fired his gun in the air as a warning.

My husband heard the shot. Someone told him that I had escaped. When he saw me, he was so angry he hit me with the butt of his .45 caliber revolver. He slapped me in front of his men. "I don't want to do this, but you force me to do it," he said. Then he hit me again, dragged me to his hut, laid me down and raped me like a savage.

I cried and cried until I fell asleep. That night, someone woke me up. It was Selya, my husband's new woman. She brought me dinner and talked to me. She said she was a school teacher, that she belonged to a well-to-do family and she fell in love with my husband.

She tried to get me involved in their organization's antigovernment activities but I showed no interest. "You can do with my husband whatever you want," I told her. "All I want is to go home to my sick child. This is the medicine for my child." I showed her the bag of medicine. "Please help me to go home," I pleaded. "I don't know if my child is still alive."

"I can't do anything for you," she shrugged. When she left me, I was in tears. I was angry and heartbroken that my own husband could do to me what the Japanese had done.

I remained a prisoner in the hut. My husband would visit me, and after a while we were on good terms again. I never asked him about Selya. But sometimes he was so nice to me that I wanted to hug him. He played the guitar and sang for me. I missed him when he was not around, and I was always eager to see him again. I felt very happy when he visited me although I did not openly show my affection or my happiness.

Sometimes he brought me breakfast, and we would talk. He said he was sorry for what he had done. I always begged him to let me go for our daughter's sake. He told me that I was brought to the mountains without his knowledge. When one of his men saw me in the drugstore, he decided to abduct me because he knew how much my husband missed me.

"I only wanted to see you and to find out about our daughters and our mothers," he said. "I was lonely. My plan was to let you go after I talked to you. But you said some harsh words, you threatened to report us to the authorities. I had to act before my men could do anything to you. I had to show my men that I was in command. But deep in my heart you are still my love. I was hurt that I had to do those things to you."

"Are you still angry with me?" he asked, holding my hands.

"So why don't you let me go?" I said. He did not answer, he just looked into my eyes. I looked at him and tried to understand what he could not say.

Then I heard a knock. One of his men brought us supper. It was dusk. We ate in silence. He smiled at me and I smiled back. It was the first time I smiled in that place.

After dinner, he put on his jacket. I knew that he was leaving. "So both of us understand each other now," he said. "You understand my situation. The time will come when we can let you go home."

I watched him leave and then lay down on my mat on the floor to sleep. I was happy now because I knew I could go. He promised me so. I felt deep in my heart that I loved him very much.

In the next three days, I did not see Doming. I asked the guard about him, but he did not answer me. Then that night, as I slept, I heard a knock. It was my husband. He slept with me that night. I did not ask him where he had been.

He got up early the following morning. We had breakfast together, and we were smiling at each other. I felt that he was happy and I was happy, too. I felt comfortable with him now, he no longer frightened me, nor did he bring back memories of my ordeal with the Japanese. I openly showed him my affection, wanting him to see that I was happy with him. But I was also worried about my mother and my children. How were they surviving without me? I was the only one who worked, and I wondered how they supported themselves now that I was away.

After some time, I knew I was pregnant again. I felt feverish, weak. I had dizzy spells. I missed my period and lost my appetite. I also had a craving for sour fruits like green mangoes and tamarind. My husband noticed that I was not feeling well. He asked about my health, but I never answered.

One day he told me he would send two of his men to bring some money to my mother's house. I thought it was useless because the men would never be able to find my mother's small house in Pasay. I pleaded with him again and knelt before him, begging him to let me go for the sake of our children.

He looked at me sadly. "I cannot let you go," he said, "because my men will vent their anger on me or on you. Since you said that you would report our activities to the military, they have completely lost their trust in you."

I was miserable. I sat in the hut, guarded by the guerrillas night and day. But one day the Army surprised us. They dropped a bomb in the area. There was a firefight between the soldiers and the guerrillas. Some of my husband's men were killed.

My husband ordered a retreat. We left the camp and walked for two days and two nights through the mountains in search of a refuge. We reached a safe place where his men built some huts from palm leaves. We slept, exhausted, but we did not eat because we had no food. The following morning, I felt a great pain in my belly. I thought I would have a miscarriage. That was the first time my husband learned that I was pregnant.

I was allowed to lie down and rest. I felt very weak. Again I pleaded with my husband. "Let me go home," I said. "How can I give birth in this mountain? What will happen to me? We have no medicine, no doctor. Please let me go." Doming remained silent. Then Selya called him. She was getting jealous about all the attention my husband was giving me.

I had been in the mountains exactly three months now. I had no chance of escaping. My nightmares began again; images of Japanese soldiers flashed in my sleep.

One morning, I was told to go to another hut for a meeting. My husband, Selya and his men were all there. Doming spoke, "Selya and three of the men will have to go to town to buy food and medicine," he said. "Rosa will come with you."

"Why me? I cannot go," I answered.

Then Selya asked, "Suppose she escapes, because now is her chance to flee?"

Doming looked at me and said, "Shoot her, if she attempts to escape. All of you—Selya and you three—if you let her escape, do not return here or I will kill you."

He ended the meeting by saying, "Tomorrow, early in the morning, you must go to the town." I went back to my hut thinking about my situation. My husband followed me. "Rosa, you must go with them," he said. "Then once you reach the town, escape for your own good."

"No, I will not go with them," I said. "I will stay here and endure the sufferings you have burdened me with. Do you want me to get killed if I try to escape?"

"Rosa, there are many soldiers in town," he said. "They cannot possibly shoot you there. Our eldest child needs you. Rosario is dead now. She died in the hospital. I sent my men to your mother's house to give some money, but she refused to take it. She said it was useless because Rosario had died. Please, for the sake of our eldest child and for the child you are bearing now, escape." He looked very sad. "Please forgive me," he said.

"If Rosario died, I cannot forgive you," I cried. "Get out of my sight, I despise you." I cursed him again and again. That was the last time I saw his face. I wept into the night and the following morning. At about four o'clock, Selya knocked on my door. It was time to go.

We walked down the mountains with the three men. They all had revolvers in their bags. As we walked, I pleaded with Selya to let me go, but she said that they would all be executed if I escaped.

We reached the town at about nine in the morning. We bought rice and vegetables.

As they were choosing some more goods to buy, I ran away and immediately boarded a bus bound for Manila. They saw me, but could not aim their guns at me because I sat next to a soldier. Then the bus left.

An hour and a half later, I reached my mother's house. I saw my two daughters playing, and I shouted with joy. I was in tears to find that Rosario was not dead. I embraced both my daughters and my mother, and told them that I thought Rosario had died.

My mother explained that she had told the men that Rosario had died because she was so angry about my disappearance. I told her what had happened to me, and she cried bitterly. She hugged me when I told her what my own husband had done to me. "Rosa, this is your fate," she said. "Always pray to God. My poor Rosa, endure your sufferings, maybe you will be happy someday."

I went back to work, doing other people's laundry and ironing their clothes. I also sewed dresses. I worked hard so that I could earn enough money to feed all of us. But I was getting very tired. I was approaching my ninth month of pregnancy. My mother told me that I should rest.

She found work as a cook for a rich family in Angeles. She left me in the care of my aunts and uncles and told me not to worry. On December 24, 1951, I went to my employer's house to ask her if I could do some ironing that day. I got paid a daily rate, and although it was nearly Christmas Eve, I thought I would do some work so we could have some money. My employer did not want me to work, but I insisted. And she agreed because she felt sorry for me.

My employer gave me light work that day. I was ironing pillowcases, underwear and curtains. At about three o'clock, I began feeling labor pains. I could not work anymore, so my employer let me go and gave me the five pesos I had earned for the day.

By the time I reached home, the pains had become more frequent. I asked my uncle Emil to fetch my aunt Laria, who was a midwife. My aunt attended to me, and I gave birth just after midnight on Christmas Day. I heard the sound of firecrackers and merrymaking. Next door, our neighbor's radio was playing "Silent Night."

"Be happy, Rosa," my aunt said. "You have a baby boy."

"Many, many thanks to you, my dear God the Father, and to you, Jesus Christ, that I survived the difficult delivery of a baby boy," I muttered. I named the boy Jesus, because he was born on Christmas Day.

My aunt washed me and my newborn child. "Rosa, be careful because you bled a lot," she said.

That afternoon my mother arrived from Angeles. When she saw me and the baby, she whispered a short prayer of thanks. She told me she had dreamt I had given birth. She said that she was not going back to Angeles, but was staying with me. She had some money because she had saved her salary. She also brought some gifts from her employer.

One week after giving birth, I went back to work ironing clothes. My mother took care of my three children, and when I saw them together, I felt happiness in my heart. I had given up all hope that I would ever see Doming again. He would find it hard to leave his men and Selya, too. I told myself that now I had to be both father and mother to my children.

Two years later, in November 1953, I heard the news on the radio: "Domingo of Sta. Cruz, Laguna, was killed in an encounter with the military in San Pablo City in Laguna." I heard that some of his men were killed as well and the others were captured. Deep in my heart I still loved my husband, and I mourned his death.

Three months later, I visited Doming's comrades in jail. I wanted to know what had happened to him. They were all surprised to see me. "You are still alive, Rosa?" one of them asked in wonder.

"When Selya and the others returned to the mountains that day, they told your husband that they had shot and killed you because you tried to escape," they told me. "He was very sad and was never the same. He was always in deep thought. Maybe he felt responsible for what had happened. He just fought the Army until he was killed."

I told them I had given birth to a baby boy and that all my three children and I were living happily with my mother. Then I returned home. I did not feel any sadness anymore. Maybe my heart had hardened after all I had been through. I wanted to cry, but no tears fell. I realized I loved Doming. I told myself I should stand on my own two feet now because no one will help me bring up my children except God and my mother.

7

SINGLE MOTHER

For seven years, I washed clothes for other people. I had three employers for whom I worked two days a week each. I began work at seven in the morning and finished at six in the evening. After a whole day of washing, I took home a bundle of clothes to iron for the night. I worked straight from eight in the evening until four the following morning. All that ironing earned me two pesos more a day.

The next day, I went to my second employer, and the whole routine began again. That was why my hands and arms were always stiff from the hard work. But I had kind employers who treated me well and gave me old clothes for my children.

While I was at work, my mother took care of my family, went to market and cooked our food. I ate most of my meals in my employers' homes. Although the work was hard, I was happy because my children were now going to school. I was also sewing dresses during the little spare time I had. My neighbors and relatives marveled at my energy. "Rosa can work like a man because she has to support a family," they said.

Sometimes I talked with my mother and recalled my wartime ordeals. But she would stop me from talking about the past. She used to put her hands on my mouth. "Rosa," she said, "Those days are past, you must look forward now. You must think of the future for your children's sake. Forget the past, bury it and forget it."

I ironed and washed clothes even on holidays. Even during the Christmas season, when people woke up early to go to the traditional dawn masses, I was up ironing. I watched the people go to church. I heard the church bells ringing and the people singing Christmas carols. I cried silently because I wanted to go to mass, too, but I had so much ironing to do.

I kept my faith in God. I knew that He would not give me suffering that I could not endure. My only wish was that He would give me the spiritual and physical strength to go on. I worked even on Christmas Eve, as people went to hear the midnight mass.

One Christmas morning, I rushed to my employer's house with my daughter to deliver the clothes I had ironed. They were going to wear them to mass that day.

I carried the dresses that hung from wire hangers while my daughter carried a box of folded clothes. We saw some friends along the way.

"Rosa, Merry Christmas," they said. "Why are you carrying all those clothes? It's a holiday."

"My employer will wear them today," I said. "God will understand that I have to work on a holy day."

My employer served my daughter and me a rich Christmas breakfast. She had many kinds of food and fruits on the table. She handed me an envelope of money as a Christmas present. She also wrapped some cheese and ham for me to take home and gave my daughter a doll. When we returned home, I was happy to see some relatives from Pampanga who had come to visit. My mother served them what I had brought, as well as food she had prepared—fried noodles and rice cakes.

One day in October 1957, I applied for work at the La Suerte cigarette factory in Pasay. The company was a partnership between American and Chinese businessmen, and it produced American brand-cigarettes like Philip Morris and Marlboro. The management did not want to accept me because my speech was

I ironed and washed clothes even on holidays.

slurred, and I would sometimes drool. But I went to the office of
the union president and begged him for a job. He talked to the
manager on my behalf. She'll be a good worker, the union president said, she will not spend all the time talking. Besides, it's her
hands that are important.

The manager relented and hired me. I did my work as best as I
could. The other workers, however, made fun of me. They imitat-
ed the way I talked. They teased me, and I became the butt of
jokes. I didn't argue with them. I just did my work.

My first job was as a sweeper in the processing section of the
factory. The raw tobacco was brought to the factory packed in big
barrels which weighed 2,000 kilograms each. The tobacco was

steamed and mixed with chemicals. It came out of the processing machine hot and steaming. Then the tobacco sheaves were unloaded on a conveyor belt, beside which women workers lined up to separate the leaves. It was my task to gather with a broom the stray tobacco leaves that fell on the floor from the conveyor belt.

I worked eight hours, from seven a.m. to four p.m., six days a week. When the other workers went on overtime, I joined them as well. Before long, I learned how to separate the tobacco leaves, and when one of the women was absent, I took her place.

When I began work, the minimum wage was only four pesos a day; it was raised to six pesos in 1966. But my family managed on my pay: one *salop* of rice, which weighs more than two kilos, cost only sixty centavos then, and it lasted us two days.

My mother died of hypertension in 1963. I felt very sad and lonely. I was thirty-six years old, my eldest daughter was sixteen. Life without my mother was difficult, as I had no one else with whom to share my past.

My mother had lived with me and my children until the end of her life. I loved her very much. We shared all the happiness and bitterness that life brought us. I loved her even more than I loved my husband.

Now that she was gone, I had no one to talk to whenever the images of the war haunted me like ghosts. Whenever I felt the need to talk, I would write instead on small sheets of paper, "Japanese soldiers raped me. They fell in line to rape me." Then I would crumple the paper and throw it away.

I reared my children to be respectful and obedient. None of them knew about their mother's wartime slavery. They knew that I loved their father. Many other men courted me, but I shunned them. I felt that they would only oppress me, that there would be more children, and they would leave me alone to care for them.

Eventually my children married. All three of them also worked in the cigarette factory, as did my two sons-in-law.

In 1969, the manager of the factory decided to recruit two women for the quality control department. I was one of those chosen to train for the job because I was a good worker. I was rarely absent because my family depended on the money I earned. I passed the training and was tasked with recording the dryness and the moisture in the fine cuts of tobacco that passed through my machine. I inspected thousands of boxes of tobacco every day. There were three of us in the quality control department. We worked three hours straight, then rested half an hour, then worked again. My eight-hour shift normally stretched to ten hours because there was always plenty of work to do.

I also learned how to apply the flavoring to the tobacco. If the operator in the flavoring section was absent, I took over. Sometimes I swept the floor as well, even if it was no longer my job. I worked in quality control eleven years, until the department was computerized. I was also getting exhausted from the work, which required tremendous concentration.

In 1981, I returned to being a sweeper. That way, I could be called on to substitute for absent workers in the other sections like flavoring and quality control. In 1985, I was made a shop steward of the processing section. When any of the workers there had problems, it was my job to present them to the management. By this time, there were nearly a hundred men in the processing section. The men had taken over from the women—there were now only a dozen or so women left.

In June 1990, when I was sixty-three and approaching retirement, I was given lighter work. My job now was to search the women workers as they left the factory. The management told me, "Now you are on our side and you have to protect our interests." So I told my fellow workers I had to do my job. I had to inspect whether they were taking things out of the factory. But it was very light work. By this time there were only six women left in the factory. The following year, I retired from La Suerte. I had worked there thirty-four years.

During that time, I fed and clothed my children and sent them to school. I also paid for the education of my grandchildren who finished high school. Even while I worked in the factory, I did some sewing on the side. When I retired from La Suerte, I received a lump sum of one hundred thirty-six thousand pesos, which I used to build concrete walls on my little house and change the rotten wood on the floor. I also bought a refrigerator and a sewing machine.

Today I live on a social security pension of about three thousand pesos a month. I use that to pay for the lease on the land on which my house stands, and for food, utility bills and other needs. My daughter Rosario and her two grown-up children live with me. We try to manage on a food budget of one hundred and fifty pesos a day. It is not always easy because food is expensive these days. I still do some laundry and some sewing whenever I can.

I now have twelve grandchildren and thirteen great-grandchildren. I am happy I have them. Without them, I would have roamed the streets like a madwoman.

8

GOING PUBLIC

One morning in June 1992, while I was hanging my laundry on the clothesline, I heard a female voice on the radio talking about women who were raped and enslaved by Japanese troops during the Second World War.

I shook all over, I felt my blood turn white. I heard that there was a group called the Task Force on Filipino Comfort Women looking for women like me. I could not forget the words that blared out of the radio that day: "Don't be ashamed, being a sex slave is not your fault. It is the responsibility of the Japanese Imperial Army. Stand up and fight for your rights."

I was to find out later that the woman speaking was Liddy Alejandro of the group Bayan. She gave a telephone number for women to call. I could not even write the number. I suddenly felt weak and tears began falling from my eyes. I dared not even look around me, for fear that people nearby would notice my unusual reaction.

I lay down on the floor of our house. Tears were blurring my eyes. My heart was beating very fast. I asked myself whether I should expose my ordeal. What if my children and relatives found me dirty and repulsive?

Everyday, I tuned in to the same radio program. At the same time, I tried to forget the announcement about comfort women.

Many weeks passed, and I did not hear the announcement again. But on September 3, 1992, a Thursday, another woman spoke. It was Nelia Sancho, and she was repeating Liddy's words. I wept in front of the radio. My daughter Rosario ran upstairs and found me sobbing.

"Mother, what happened?" she asked. "Why are you crying?" I could not answer. I only pointed to the radio. Nelia was still speaking and announcing a number to call. "I am that woman she is talking about," I said. Rosario hugged me. It was the first time she learned about what had been done to me.

I asked my daughter if she would accept a mother who had been a sex slave. "I love you so much, it does not matter that you have a dark past," she said.

With Rosario's reassurance, I made up my mind. I told her to write a letter to radio station DZXL, addressed to Ducky Paredes, who was the host of the program. This is the letter she wrote:

> *Dear Mr. Paredes, I heard a woman talking about sex slaves in your radio program. I am Maria Rosa Luna Henson, who was made a sex slave during the Second World War. Please give me the telephone number of that woman's office. I will wait for your answer on the radio. Just call me Lola Rosa on the air.*
>
> *Respectfully,*
> *Lola Rosa*

The following week, on September 10, 1992, my radio was tuned in to the same program. Paredes was on the air. "Lola Rosa, I know that you are listening at this moment," he said. Then he gave a telephone number. "Ask for Liddy or Nelia," he said.

That afternoon, I went to the pay telephone in my neighbor's store. But I turned back, for fear that they would overhear me. That night, I could not sleep. What would happen if I went public? Is it not shameful to recall what I had been through? What would people say?

In the end, I thought it was time to let go of the burden in my heart.

At about 1:30 p.m. the following day, a Friday, I placed a call in my neighbor's phone. It was Liddy who answered. "Are you Lola Rosa?" she asked.

"Yes, I am Maria Rosa Luna Henson," I said. They wanted to see me, so I gave them instructions to fetch me in front of the bakery near where I live. I said I would be wearing a printed red dress. They came the following morning. I was waiting with Rosario. Gigi, a member of the Task Force on Filipino Comfort Women, and her husband fetched me.

They brought Rosario and me to Liddy's office, about an hour away from where I live. I told Liddy my story, and later Nelia, who interviewed me on tape. I was in tears as I told my story. It was very difficult for me to relate what I had been through. But it was also a great relief. I felt like a heavy weight had been removed from my shoulders, as if thorns had been pulled out of my grieving heart. I felt I had recovered my long-lost strength and self-esteem.

I felt better when I returned home. I kept asking Rosario if she still respected me even after she heard the secret that I had kept for fifty years. "I love you even more," she answered.

Four days later, on September 17, I heard a knocking on our door. It was late, close to eleven p.m. I was still up, washing clothes, which I still do to earn some extra money. I opened the door to find Nelia and three other staff members of the Task Force on Filipino Comfort Women.

They spoke to me about coming out in public. "That is very difficult for me to do," I said, "because I only got in touch with you to ease my heart."

But Nelia's colleague, Indai Sajor, pleaded with me. "Maybe there are other women like you who are still alive. If they hear your appeal, they would also come out in public."

They told me there was going to be a press conference the following day, and they asked me to be there. They also asked me to draft a short message to the government, asking for support for Filipino comfort women.

In the end, I understood their explanations and gave in to their request. I felt happy and at ease with myself. I realized I had a responsibility to come out with my story. There were others like me, and they, like me, needed to have a measure of justice before they died. I also wanted to make the younger generation aware about the evils of war.

On September 18, 1992, I gave my very first press conference. Many local and foreign reporters were there. That was also the first time I met Romeo Capulong, who was introduced to me as a human rights lawyer. The reporters asked me many questions, and I could not stop my tears as I answered them. As I told my story, images of Japanese soldiers falling in line to rape me kept returning to my mind.

The day after the press conference, my photograph was all over the newspapers. I heard myself on the radio and saw myself on television. That was the first time my two other children—Rosalinda and Jesus—found out about my past. They saw my photograph in the newspaper, and they both cried when they read my story. They came to see me the same day. They hugged me and said, "We love you. If it weren't for you, we would not be here."

What followed was a series of press conferences. I spoke in radio stations and was invited to testify in the Senate about my experiences. Capulong accompanied me as my lawyer. On September 25, 1992, I joined other members of the Task Force on Filipino Comfort Women in a march to Mendiola Bridge demanding justice for comfort women. I also marched in front of the Japanese embassy, and submitted a letter to then Prime Minister Keichi Miyazawa, asking him to pay heed to the plight of Filipino comfort women.

Three weeks after I came out in public, another woman, Gertrudes Balisalisa, went to the Task Force to say that she had also been forced into sexual slavery during the Second World War. She, too, came out publicly, appealing to other women to come forth with their stories.

I did not meet her and four other former comfort women until October 28, 1992, when Nelia brought all of us together in a house in Quezon City. Gertrudes saw me as I entered. She got up and embraced me. "Lola Rosa," she said tearfully, "you are my inspiration." I hugged her back and said, "I am so happy you, too, came out with your story."

I met the other women—Lola Atanacia Cortez, Amonita Balahadja, Tomasa Salinog and Francisca Macabebe. We had dinner together, after which we sat around to tell each other our stories. I listened closely to what they had to say. Their stories made me very sad. I saw that we had many bitter and painful experiences in common.

Their stories firmed up my decision to go public. I realized that my role was to serve as an example to other survivors of wartime sex slavery who may still be ashamed to come out with their experience.

It was not an easy decision to make. I often heard people in our neighborhood and elsewhere sneering at me behind my back. "You just want to be a superstar or to make money," they said. The taunts seemed endless. But I found support from people who understood my case. My children, too, were very supportive.

The public was generally sympathetic to me. But there were times when people were also mean. In late 1992, I attended a forum at a five-star hotel. Prominent women in the government and the media were there. After I shared my story, one of the women journalists there stood up and spoke in a loud voice. She accused me of going public with my story only because I wanted to make plenty of money. I cried. At that moment, I regretted having come out with my story at all.

Even my fourteen-year-old granddaughter Tina was not spared. She was teased by the neighbors, one of whom showed her my photograph which came out in a newspaper. "Is this your *lola*?" he taunted her. "She must have been quite strong to service battalions of soldiers."

Tina cried and confronted me. "Why did you come out public-ly, *Lola*? I now have to fight with the neighbors who keep teasing me."

"You must not do that," I tried to appease her. "They do not know what happened during the war. I have to come out so they will know and understand."

I felt my heart break when I told her this. Whenever I was down, I went to the Task Force office to cry. I was able to sur-mount all this pain because I had the support of my family and of the Task Force members. I am happy that my children have come to accept my past. And in the different countries I have visited since, people I have met have been very sympathetic. Many of them have come to me and said, "I will pray for you, so that you can have justice."

By November 1992, about thirty comfort women had come out publicly. The Task Force office was very busy. There were jour-nalists, lawyers, even members of the Japanese Diet who came to visit. At about this time, we talked about the possibility of filing a lawsuit in Japan. We discussed the matter with the other comfort women, Task Force members, some lawyers and sympathetic Jap-anese activists.

On December 2, 1992, I made my first trip to Japan to attend a forum on war compensation for comfort women. I went with Indai Sajor, one of the leaders of the Task Force. I spoke in several forums, where I met Korean, Chinese, Taiwanese and Dutch comfort women who were also there. Through an interpreter, we learned about each other's experiences. We hugged each other and cried.

One of the Korean women, Kang Soon-Ae, told us that she was taken from her home in April 1941, even before the Pacific War broke out. She was then only fourteen years old. She was taken to various places by the Japanese Army, including China and Palau, in the South Pacific. She spent six years of her youth as a comfort woman.

When Kang Soon-Ae found out that I was born on December 5, 1927, she cried out in surprise and said, "We are twins." She was born on the same day as I.

I also met Lee Kwi-bun, another Korean woman who was raped by Japanese soldiers for six years in a comfort station. On weekends, she said, up to a hundred soldiers lined up to rape her. She cried as she told me her story, and she held my hands. She told me that after the war, she became a beggar. She walked a long distance back to her home, begging for alms along the way.

The high point of this trip was a meeting where former comfort women from various countries gave testimonies about their war experiences. The audience included members of non-government organizations and some United Nations officials.

During my stay, I met many Japanese—activists, journalists, university professors, lawyers and church people. They welcomed me and sympathized with me. They were warm and welcoming, so unlike the Japanese soldiers I had encountered fifty years ago.

I returned to Japan to file a lawsuit in the district court of Tokyo on April 2, 1993. Ours was a class suit with eighteen plaintiffs, all comfort women. We were assisted by a panel of Japanese lawyers. I went there with another comfort woman, Julia Porras. I also met a Korean woman who was filing a lawsuit similar to ours. Our suit demanded an apology and some compensation from the Japanese government.

All throughout my stay in Japan, I was worrying about my house. On the evening of March 31, 1993, on the eve of our departure for Tokyo, my small, two-story house burned down. I was then at the office of the Task Force. My daughter Rosario was at home, but she was not able to save anything. All that I had worked and saved for in over thirty years were lost in the fire—my television set, china, refrigerator, two sewing machines.

I had to stay temporarily with my son, but his house was too small to accommodate all of us. I moved to an elementary school near our area and stayed there a month while we slowly rebuilt our house from scrap materials. I received some donations from Japanese and Filipino friends and that helped. I was grateful that in my twilight years, I had friends whom I could rely on. I built a very simple structure that looks like a garage, a one-room affair with concrete walls and an iron roof.

The days passed very quickly. In April 1993, I went to Davao to help the Task Force set up a network there. I came out on television and radio, calling for former comfort women to come out with their ordeal. I met with different people and helped sew Maria Clara dresses for four comfort women who were scheduled to leave for Japan.

In September 1993, I went to Berlin for an international conference on women, war and rape. I met more Korean former comfort women and two former comfort women from the Netherlands. I stayed in Germany a week, then returned to Manila in time for a rally in front of the Japanese Embassy that was attended by thirty other comfort women.

The next month, I returned to Japan for the first hearing of the Tokyo District Court. I testified in the court room about what had happened to me in the hands of the Japanese. Another Filipino comfort woman, Tomasa Salinog, also testified.

We spoke in several forums. Every time we spoke, Tomasa and I cried because we remembered all that had happened to us. Images of Japanese soldiers would flash before my mind whenever I recalled my wartime ordeal.

After the forums, we would return to our rooms exhausted. There were times I wept alone in my room. I thought that we had to go through so much just to be able to get justice.

While we were in Osaka, I fell ill. The doctor checked my blood pressure and told me to rest. My blood pressure had shot up from fatigue. I realized I needed to take things easy or my health would deteriorate. The other comfort women also suffered from illnesses. Two from the Visayas had already died.

I decided to take a leave from active work in the Task Force. I thought it was best to stay home for a while, to rest and just live a quiet life. Some of the Task Force members continued to visit me, and I still gave occasional interviews to journalists and visitors from Japan.

I became active again in 1994 when Tomiichi Murayama, the new Japanese prime minister, brought out the idea of establishing a center for Asian women in lieu of compensation for comfort women. I thought that this idea was far from what we had demanded. I felt disappointed. Such a center, which was supposed to give training to women, would not benefit the comfort women, who were already old.

Even the proposal to course the compensation through official development aid was not a good one. To my mind, this kind of aid did not benefit ordinary people. Much of it went to corrupt government officials.

The comfort women demanded genuine compensation to themselves as individuals, not a mechanism that would give the money to the government or a private group.

In the end of August 1994, Murayama visited the Philippines. We thought he might bring up with President Fidel V. Ramos the idea of creating a women's center. So we planned a rally. Murayama arrived on a rainy Monday. About fifty of us, mainly former comfort women, staged a picket in front of the Manila Hotel where the prime minister stayed. It was raining hard, and we were drenched. After half an hour, the police drove us away from the hotel.

One of the former comfort women who attended the rally that day was Simplicia Marilag. She was not feeling well, and the rain made things worse. She said she was dizzy, and she had chills. We took her back home, but a few days later, she died.

The Japanese government insists that the issue of compensation had already been resolved when it paid reparations to the Philippine government after the end of the Second World War. I do not agree with this position. Through all these years, I have never received compensation of any kind. I had to work hard to support myself and my family. I think it is the Japanese government's duty to acknowledge its past sins and to pay.

Many have asked me whether I am still angry with the Japanese. Maybe it helped that I have faith. I had learned to accept suffering. I also learned to forgive. If Jesus Christ could forgive those who crucified Him, I thought I could also find it in my heart to forgive those who had abused me. Half a century had passed. Maybe my anger and resentment were no longer as fresh. Telling my story has made it easier for me to be reconciled with the past.

But I am still hoping to see justice done before I die.

CHRONOLOGY

April 15, 1907—My mother Julia was born in Angeles, Pampanga.

1920—Julia begins to work as a servant in the Henson household.

September 1927—Julia's family transfers to Pasay.

December 5, 1927—I was born in Pasay.

1931—I meet my father for the first time.

December 8, 1941—Pearl Harbor is bombed.

February 1942—I was raped by a Japanese officer and two soldiers in Fort McKinley.

March 1942—My mother and I return to Angeles, Pampanga.

April 1943—I am held by Japanese soldiers and forced to become a comfort woman.

January 1944—I am rescued by the Hukbalahap from the Japanese garrison.

March 1944—I regain consciousness and begin a slow recovery.

January 27, 1945—The Allied Forces liberate Pampanga.

September 1945—Domingo and I get married.

August 1947—I give birth to Rosario.

September 1949—My second child, Rosalinda, is born.

May 1950—My husband is abducted by armed men.

March 1951—I am abducted by the HMB and brought to their camp in the mountains.

July 1951—I escape from the guerrillas.

December 1951—My youngest child, Jesus, is born.

1954—My husband is shot by Philippine Army soldiers.

1957—I begin work at the La Suerte cigarette factory.

August 1963—My mother Julia dies.

1991—I retire from La Suerte.

June 30, 1992—I hear on the radio an announcement about comfort women.

September 3, 1992—I hear a second radio announcement asking comfort women to come out in public.

September 11, 1992—I call the Task Force on Filipino Comfort Women.

September 12, 1992—I tell my story for the first time to members of the Task Force.

September 18, 1992—My first press conference as a comfort woman.

December 1992—I testify at an international public hearing on war compensation held in Tokyo, Japan.

April 1, 1993—With other comfort women, I file a lawsuit demanding compensation from the Japanese government at the district court of Tokyo.

1996—Maria Rosa Henson's memoir, *Comfort Woman: Slave of Destiny*, is published by the Philippine Center for Investigative Journalism.

1996—Maria Rosa Henson accepts compensation from the Asian Women's Fund, a private fund organized by the Japanese Government. The money was offered to the victims as "atonement payments," rather than representing any official acknowledgment of responsibility. She was the first to accept unofficial compensation from the Japanese, although she was adamant in the belief that they owed her official indemnity as well.

August 18, 1997—Maria Rosa Henson dies of a heart attack at age sixty-nine. She is buried in the saya with an autumn-leaf design that she made herself and wore to her book launch a year earlier.

Asian Voices
An Asia/Pacific/Perspectives Series
Series Editor: Mark Selden

Identity and Resistance in Okinawa by Matthew Allen
Tales of Tibet: Sky Burials, Prayer Wheels, and Wind Horses edited and translated by Herbert J. Batt, foreword by Tsering Shakya
Tiananmen Moon: Inside the Chinese Student Uprising of 1989, Twenty-fifth Anniversary Edition by Philip J Cunningham
Voicing Concerns: Contemporary Chinese Critical Inquiry edited by Gloria Davies, conclusion by Geremie Barmé
The Subject of Gender: Daughters and Mothers in Urban China by Harriet Evans
Peasants, Rebels, Women, and Outcastes: The Underside of Modern Japan by Mikiso Hane
Comfort Woman: A Filipina's Story of Prostitution and Slavery under the Japanese Military by Maria Rosa Henson, introduction by Yuki Tanaka
Japan's Past, Japan's Future: One Historian's Odyssey by Ienaga Saburō, translated and introduced by Richard H. Minear
I'm Married to Your Company! Everyday Voices of Japanese Women by Masako Itoh, edited by Nobuko Adachi and James Stanlaw
Sisters and Lovers: Women and Desire in Bali by Megan Jennaway
Moral Politics in a South Chinese Village: Responsibility, Reciprocity, and Resistance by Hok Bun Ku
Queer Japan from the Pacific War to the Internet Age by Mark McLelland
Behind the Silence: Chinese Voices on Abortion by Nie Jing-Bao
Rowing the Eternal Sea: The Life of a Minamata Fisherman by Oiwa Keibo, narrated by Ogata Masato, translated by Karen Colligan-Taylor
The Scars of War: Tokyo during World War II, Writings of Takeyama Michio edited and translated by Richard H. Minear
War and Conscience in Japan: Nambara Shigeru and the Asia-Pacific War edited and translated by Richard H. Minear
Growing Up Untouchable in India: A Dalit Autobiography by Vasant Moon, translated by Gail Omvedt, introduction by Eleanor Zelliot
Exodus to North Korea: Shadows from Japan's Cold War by Tessa Morris-Suzuki
Hiroshima: The Autobiography of Barefoot Gen by Nakazawa Keiji, edited and translated by Richard H. Minear
China Ink: The Changing Face of Chinese Journalism by Judy Polumbaum
Red Is Not the Only Color: Contemporary Chinese Fiction on Love and Sex between Women, Collected Stories edited by Patricia Sieber
Sweet and Sour: Life-Worlds of Taipei Women Entrepreneurs by Scott Simon
Dear General MacArthur: Letters from the Japanese during the American Occupation by Sodei Rinjirō, edited by John Junkerman, translated by Shizue Matsuda, foreword by John W. Dower

Unbroken Spirits: Nineteen Years in South Korea's Gulag by Suh Sung, translated by Jean Inglis, foreword by James Palais

No Time for Dreams: Living in Burma under Military Rule by Carolyn Wakeman and San San Tin

A Thousand Miles of Dreams: The Journeys of Two Chinese Sisters by Sasha Su-Ling Welland

Dancing in Shadows: Sihanouk, the Khmer Rouge, and the United Nations in Cambodia by Benny Widyono

Voices Carry: Behind Bars and Backstage during China's Revolution and Reform by Ying Ruocheng and Claire Conceison